Juan Marichal

Juan Marichal

My Journey from the
Dominican Republic
to Cooperstown

By Juan Marichal and Lew Freedman

MVP
BOOKS

First published in 2011 by MVP Books, an imprint of MBI Publishing Company and the Quayside Publishing Group, 400 First Avenue North, Suite 300, Minneapolis, MN 55401 USA

MVP Books titles are also available at discounts in bulk quantity for industrial or sales-promotional use. For details write to Special Sales Manager at MBI Publishing Company, 400 First Avenue North, Suite 300, Minneapolis, MN 55401 USA.

To find out more about our books, visit us online at www.mvpbooks.com.

Library of Congress Cataloging-in-Publication Data

Marichal, Juan.

Juan Marichal : my journey from the Dominican Republic to Cooperstown / Juan Marichal with Lew Freedman.

  p. cm.

ISBN 978-0-7603-4059-2 (hardbound w/jkt)

1. Marichal, Juan. 2. Baseball players—Dominican Republic—Biography. I. Title.

GV865.M335A3 2011

796.357092--dc22

[B]

2011009176

Printed in the United States of America

Editor: Josh Leventhal
Design Manager: Brenda C. Canales
Layout Designer: Danielle Smith
Cover Designer: Diana Boger

Front cover photo by Focus on Sport/Getty Images.

To God, for giving me this talent,
for giving me the certainty that nothing is impossible.

To my mother, for showing me love and happiness.

To the love of my life, my soulmate, my rock, Alma Rosa,
for helping me fullfill my dream.

To my beloved children, grandchildren, and great-granddaughter.
All of you have brought so much joy to my life.

To my country. I am one proud Dominican Dandy.

To anyone and everyone I ever met through baseball,
you helped shape me into who I am.

Last but not least, to my fans—thank you for the memories!

Contents

Introduction
by Lew Freedman

Just before the ball flew out of his right hand hurtling toward home plate, Juan Marichal's left foot kicked high in the air with the ease of a chorus-line dancer. That rare twist to his motion gave the pride of the Dominican Republic one of the most distinctive pitching styles in Major League Baseball history.

A batter trying to pick up the seams on the ball in order to read the pitch instead saw this foot right in his face (or so it seemed), and his concentration was broken. Most likely, the hitter swung and missed or made an out. Marichal's kicking was so high, sometimes it seemed that it would throw him over backwards, yet somehow he managed to remain upright.

But more than just unique and disorienting, Marichal had pinpoint control and a range of effective pitches that set the future Hall of Famer apart from most hurlers. In a major league career spanning 1960 to 1975, Marichal was simply hard to beat. He was better than 95 percent of the pitchers in history. He was among the elite of the elite.

Born on October 20, 1937, in the Dominican Republic town of Laguna Verde, where his family farmed, Juan Marichal was a sensation as a teenager and a superstar as he matured. Although he briefly played with the Boston Red Sox and Los Angeles Dodgers, Marichal remains identified with his long-term team, the San Francisco Giants.

During his playing days, Marichal won 243 games—the most by a Latin American pitcher until Dennis Martinez surpassed him in 1998—and compiled a lifetime 2.89 earned run average, among the finest marks of all time. Marichal was selected for the All-Star Game 10 times, was named Most Valuable Player of the midsummer classic in 1965, and pitched a no-hitter in 1963. Marichal pitched in one World Series, against the New York Yankees in 1962.

One of the greatest pitchers of his era, Marichal hooked up in memorable duels with the few other National League hurlers who were at his superstar level: Sandy Koufax, Warren Spahn, Don Drysdale, and Bob Gibson. It was Marichal, though, who with 191 victories won more games than any other pitcher in the 1960s. In June 1966, *Time* magazine spread out nine pictures of Marichal on its cover, accompanied by the phrase "The Best Right Arm in Baseball."

Less known for the flat-out speed of his fastball, Marichal was more a master of control who baffled batters with a mix of speeds, pitches, and deliveries. They never knew where the ball was coming from or how it would arrive.

Although he was supervisor of the Oakland Athletics' scouting operation for 14 years, Marichal remains most closely aligned with the Giants and such star teammates as Willie Mays, Willie McCovey, Monte Irvin, and Jim Davenport.

Growing up, Marichal did not live in luxury on the family property. Although they grew enough crops for everyone to have enough to eat, the home had neither running water nor electricity. Juan's passion was always baseball, and he counted among his childhood friends the Alou brothers—Felipe, Matty, and Jesus—all future major leaguers. They became the first all-brother outfield while playing for the Giants, and Marichal remains as close as a fourth brother to them.

He also remains close to his old employer, the Giants. In 2010, following the team's surprising run to the National League pennant, Marichal was thrilled to be part of the festivities and to witness his old affiliation's moment of glory as the club captured its first World Series title since 1954 (when the team was still located in New York). The Giants brought Marichal and the team's other living Hall of Famers to the Series home opener to throw out the ceremonial first pitch. It was a great thrill for the old pitcher to see the enthusiasm and ultimate triumph displayed by his underdog club.

Marichal is a national hero in the Dominican Republic. Friendly with several recent presidents of his native country, he is one of the most prominent and popular people on an island that is just a short plane hop from the United States and abuts Haiti along the countries' mountainous border. A father of six, Marichal has been married to wife, Alma, since 1962.

Marichal emerged from Laguna Verde obscurity as a gangly teenager. He was inducted into the Air Force in Santo Domingo to play baseball and was ordered by dictator Rafael Trujillo and son Ramfis to play for their team in the capital rather than in his home area.

But Marichal was soon liberated from the Dominican national team by a Giants offer that took him to the minor leagues in 1958. In the United States, he gradually learned English and was treated courteously and kindly by families he boarded with in minor league towns. However, he also encountered discrimination because of his dark skin and his reliance on Spanish as his first language.

In the late 1950s, Latin American players were rare in organized baseball in the United States. But during the subsequent decade, players such as Marichal, Roberto Clemente, the Alou brothers, and others helped jump-start a revolution that has transformed the sport. They were pioneers, at the forefront of baseball's open-door policy to Latins that a half century later has resulted in an explosion of participation in the States (today, about one out of every four major league players are of Latin American origins), helped elevate the sport to greater heights of popularity throughout Latin America, and produced dozens of all-stars.

For Marichal, the journey culminated with election to the National Baseball Hall of Fame in 1983. He has long been a role model to young Hispanic players, and his name remains in front of Dominican and other Latin American fans through his work first as minister of sport in the Dominican Republic and as a Spanish-language broad-caster of postseason baseball for ESPN Deportes.

Marichal's life has not been completely free of controversy. In the heat of an intense Giants–Dodgers game in 1965, an argument with Los Angeles catcher Johnny Roseboro turned ugly and Marichal infamously swung his bat and hit Roseboro in the head. For such a normally long-fused man who never engaged in acts born of temper, it was a stunning mistake in judgment and forever tainted his otherwise perfect record of behavior on the diamond.

This brief moment of hot-headedness was an inexplicable departure from the norm in an exemplary life and has haunted Marichal for years. Most of the time, he was a gracious playing partner to both teammates and opposing players. Blessed with a sunny disposition, Marichal refers to men he has played with and known away from the field as "gentlemen." It is just about the highest compliment he can offer. It is equally true that it could be turned around and applied to Marichal himself. That is how he strikes people, the impression he leaves, that he is always a gentleman.

Marichal's major league career began dramatically. As a rookie in July 1960, he nearly pitched a no-hitter in his first game. He also engaged in one of the most famous pitching duels of the second half of the 20th century when he and fellow Hall of Famer Warren Spahn battled for 16 innings in a scoreless tie before Marichal won the game, 1–0.

After he was elected to the Hall of Fame, Marichal had his No. 27 jersey retired by the Giants. In 1998, he was chosen by the *Sporting News* as one of the 100 Greatest Baseball Players of all time.

After Marichal's retirement as Athletics scouting director in 1998, he more and more embraced his identity as one of the Giants' greatest players and became more involved with the team that first brought him to the majors. After the Giants built a new ballpark in 2000, replacing the quirky Candlestick Park where Marichal spent most of his career, the team erected a statue of the pitcher, depicting him in his classic, high-kick pitching pose.

Getting elected to the Hall of Fame in 1983 is Marichal's most precious memory in baseball. On a hot day in Cooperstown, New York, Marichal spoke of the pleasure of being chosen and representing not only the Giants, but the Dominican Republic.

"I accept this honor on behalf of my family, my country, and everyone who helped make my baseball career a reality," Marichal told the cheering crowd after admitting he was very nervous.

Marichal's has been an extraordinary life. He grew up in circumstances that would brand his family a member of the lower class economically. He has risen to international fame because of the strength of his pitching arm. However, he is an accessible celebrity in the Dominican, where the biggest fear when he goes out in public is that he will be mobbed because of his fame.

A street is named after him in Santo Domingo, and if he attends the winter league games of his favorite local team, Leones del Escogido (the Escogido Lions), at Estadio Quisqueya he is treated as an honored guest, escorted to a box seat near the home dugout often with team officials. Security officials protect him from his eager and adoring fans so he can watch the games in peace. Still, if fans come close, he usually waves security away in order to talk with them and sign autographs.

Whether in the ballpark or in the street, heads swivel when Marichal walks past, and whispers can be overheard, "There's Juan Marichal."

On the short walk from his car to the ballpark entrance one night, Marichal was recognized by many fans. Some waved. Some called his name. A few asked for autographs, and one particularly bold and energetic young woman asked to pose for a photo with him outside the park.

There is some talk that the old park, which houses two Santo Domingo teams, is going to be replaced by a new one that will also embrace a sprawling shopping complex, a hotel, and perhaps other development. The talk is that the new park will be named after Juan Marichal.

It would be a fitting cap to Marichal's baseball life. His individual accomplishments on the diamond made him one of the greatest of all time. He maintains a close relationship with his favorite major league team. He is a hero in his home country. He has a happy and good family life. And as a broadcaster, he maintains a fulfilling connection to his favorite sport.

Now in his 70s, Marichal can look back at a life well lived, one that included certain amounts of adversity but has overall been a very happy one. He has been an unknown, a pioneer, a star, and an exemplar placed on a pedestal.

As he looks back, even at the trying times, Juan Marichal does so in good cheer, making no excuses for his mistakes, rare though they are, and with deep pride over his successes. He can look around the private room attached to his spacious downtown Santo Domingo home and reach out and touch the physical symbols of a distinguished career.

The walls are decorated with photographs of Marichal standing with fellow Hall of Famers and other ballplayers, with pictures of Marichal posing with presidents of the Dominican Republic and the United States, with artwork of Marichal in mid-throw, that leg kicked so high, his body tilted, his right arm nearly dragging on the ground. There are glass cases with special autographed bats and balls from other Hall of Famers. There are shelves filled with baseball memorabilia. Almost lost amidst the souvenirs and comfortable chairs and couch is a television set. Marichal watches a lot of baseball on TV, and this is where he watches.

It is humorous to apply the term "man cave" to Marichal's hideaway, but even if the description is more typically applied to places where much younger men drink beer and have friends over to yell at the screen, it serves the purpose. Elsewhere in the house, the wall decorations are paintings by Dominican artists and have more likely been hung by Alma. This is Juan's room, Juan's special place.

This is a baseball room, a mini Juan Marichal museum. It was an appropriate place for Marichal to sit for hours and reflect upon his life and career. Moments of youth can never be replicated, but surrounded by reminders of how it was, Marichal was able to re-create experiences from long ago, and talk about how it was.

CHAPTER 1

A Stunning Debut

*J*uan Marichal was introduced to San Francisco Giants fans on the night of July 19, 1960. The date of his first start in the major leagues is one he always remembers, not least of all because it may have been the greatest pitching debut of any player in history.

The lanky right-handed thrower from the Dominican Republic had been promoted to the Giants' roster from the franchise's AAA affiliate in Tacoma, Washington, just nine days earlier. Now he was scheduled to face the Philadelphia Phillies at Candlestick Park, his new home field. As he was driven to the ballpark by his old and dear friend and fellow Dominican Felipe Alou, the rookie felt no nervousness. He was emotional, but it was a controlled excitement, a readiness to demonstrate his ability at the top level of the sport, to prove that he belonged in the majors.

The starting pitcher huddled in the clubhouse with his catcher, Hobie Landrith, before the game to review the opposing lineup. Landrith asked Marichal if he was at all familiar with the tendencies of the Philadelphia hitters. Marichal told him that he had never seen any of the Phillies batters before, that in fact he had never seen a major league game before that week, except on television.

Landrith decided to identify the Phillies' starters by the numbers on their uniforms rather than by their names, since none of the names meant anything to Marichal.

The Phillies were not one of the more powerful teams in the National League at the time, but they did have some dangerous hitters and old pros in the lineup. Shortstop Ruben Amaro led off. Second baseman Tony Taylor followed. Johnny Callison, a very solid hitter playing right field, batted third, and first baseman Pancho Herrera was the cleanup hitter. Right-hander John Buzhardt was Marichal's counterpart on the mound for Philadelphia.

The Giants featured a much more powerful lineup, anchored by future Hall of Famers Orlando Cepeda and Willie Mays along with the steady Jim Davenport at third base.

Not one of those Giants teammates, manager Tom Sheehan, the coaches, the fans, or Marichal himself could have expected what was to follow. When the rookie took the mound for his first start, 13,279 fans offered polite applause. Two hours and seven minutes later, they provided a standing ovation.

In a truly remarkable debut performance, Marichal pitched the full nine innings, completing a shutout and allowing just one hit while walking one and striking out 12.

The Giants took a 1–0 lead in the second inning when Mays singled, stole second base, and scored on a single by outfielder Willie Kirkland. They extended the lead to 2–0 in the fifth. Meanwhile, those Phillies batters, those strangers, one after the other stepped into the batter's box and flailed at thin air. In his first major league appearance, Marichal pitched a perfect game through six innings. He set down the first 19 batters in a row, until with one out in the seventh, Giants shortstop Eddie Bressoud committed an error to allow the Phillies' first base runner.

It was not until the eighth inning, when Philadelphia backup catcher Clay Dalrymple stroked a pinch-hit single, that the no-hit spell was broken. And then Marichal finished out the game.

Marichal's mix of fastballs, curveballs, screwballs, and sliders made the Phillies the first victims of what would be a Hall of Fame career. Philadelphia was the first major league club to be confronted by one of the most unorthodox and quirky pitching deliveries in history. Marichal leaned backwards, almost as if he might fall over, and thrust his front foot into the air high over his head. What seemed unnatural to others came naturally to Marichal, and if his kick disrupted batters' concentration, so much the better.

In a post-game press conference, sportswriters asked Marichal if he had said anything to Dalrymple when he broke up the no-hitter. "Dalrymple?" Marichal asked, puzzled. He still did not know the players' names. "Oh, the catcher for them," he added.

"What did you say to him?" a reporter asked.

"Nothing," Marichal said. "I do not know him."

THE GIANTS CALLED ME UP TO THE BIG-LEAGUE TEAM ON JULY 10. WHEN I GOT TO THE CLUBHOUSE, FELIPE ALOU AND Orlando Cepeda seemed to be very happy, very proud to have another Latin American on the club.

They took me around and introduced me to every player in the clubhouse. I was there. I was in the majors. I remember putting my uniform on and all that. When I shook all the players' hands and went to my locker, I thought I was in heaven.

Oh, my God, it was something to remember.

I had been to spring training with many of these players, but now I was really going to be on the same team. I was a teammate. I was a teammate of Willie Mays. I kept saying to myself, "Oh my God, the biggest baseball player ever and I am going to be his teammate and he is going to be playing behind me." That was something special to be on the same field with all those guys, Willie Mays, Orlando Cepeda, Felipe Alou, Willie McCovey.

When the Giants called me up from Tacoma, I met with the manager, Tom Sheehan. He was the temporary manager who took over after they fired Bill Rigney. Sheehan came up to me and said, "Juan, you're going to pitch batting practice until we get home. Then you're going to pitch the first game of the series against Philadelphia, on July 19." I said, "Yes, Mr. Sheehan, I will be prepared." So I was there pitching batting practice for a week.

I always worked hard to be in top shape. One thing I have always said is that the only way you can give 100 percent in any sport is if you are prepared to be in top shape. Otherwise, forget it. You can't give 100 percent. So I wanted to be sure I was in top shape.

The night before my debut I was feeling very excited. I couldn't wait. I wanted daylight to come for me to be on that baseball field and have my first game in the major leagues. Night games at Candlestick Park started at eight o'clock in those days. I got there at four o'clock.

On the days that I pitched I would go out for the first session for batting practice, and that's what I did before my first game. The regulars let me hit first. I hit just one or two times, and then I bunted a few times and went back into the clubhouse to get prepared. I was so anxious that day. It was a big moment.

Hobie Landrith was the catcher, and he knew it was my first game. He had to tell me about the Phillies hitters. After that I went out to the field to warm up. I was throwing and throwing and throwing and throwing. When they announced the lineup and got to my name, something went through my body that I had never felt before. Never in my life.

I was so chilled. I said to myself, "Oh my God, what is this? What is happening to me?" I never had that feeling before. I was worried that if this thing didn't go away, I couldn't pitch. There was no way I could pitch like that.

They announced the lineups. They played the national anthem. The players walked onto the field, and I walked all the way from the bullpen to the mound. The batboy was with me. When we got to the mound he took my towel and my warm-up jacket. I gave them to him and I still felt that chill. I thought this sensation was bad. I guess it was nerves, but I had never felt that before.

I threw the warm-up pitches, and when the first batter came up and the umpire yelled "Play ball!" the whole thing went away. I was back to being myself. It was a good thing that happened because, the way I had been feeling, there was no way I could pitch. When I saw that man at bat, I was fine. Then I started pitching, and I pitched very well. I had good command on every pitch. I was using all of my pitches and everything was working.

One inning, I think it was before starting the sixth, when I had 15 men in a row out, Willie Mays jogged past the mound to center field and said, "Keep it going."

The game went quickly, inning after inning. They pinch-hit one player, Tony Curry, and I got him out. Then they pinch-hit Clay Dalrymple. Tom Sheehan came out to the mound from the bench. Orlando came over from first base. They told me that this guy was a good fastball hitter and not to throw him a fastball.

I think Dalyrmple knew what they were saying to me because the first pitch I threw was a breaking ball and he was waiting for it. He hit one of those over the infield, just dropped it into the outfield. That was it, the first hit. They call that kind of hit "a dying quail." So that was my only hit of my first game in the major leagues. I pitched a one-hitter and I hardly knew any of the players, only Tony Taylor, who was from Cuba, and Ruben Amaro, who was from Mexico. I didn't know anything about any of the other Phillies until later. Johnny Callison, he was a good hitter.

It was unbelievable. I have never heard of any other pitcher whose first game was like that, one hit allowed and 12 strikeouts.

After the game my teammates were happy, for them and for me. They hugged me and then they threw one of those pies with cream in my face. They got me.

People said, "Oh man, you should have pitched a no-hitter." I said, "I only gave up one hit." I thought it was a great start. It could hardly be better. Pitching a game like that, it gave me great confidence. It showed me I could pitch in the major leagues.

This first game was so important. It established me. I knew then that I belonged with the Giants and that I wouldn't have to go back to the minor leagues. For years I had told my mother that I would be a baseball player. I used to tease her. I said, "Mama, I promise you I'm going to be a baseball player." Now I really was one.

I went home to the Dominican after the season, and I knew that my 6–2 record in my first year—it was actually half a year with the Giants—would get me on the team the next year without worry.

My mother used to say that you could not make money playing baseball, but I was going to show her that I could. When I went home after that season she was very happy. I think she started to like baseball then.

CHAPTER 2

Growing Up in the Dominican Republic

In the Dominican Republic, which shares the island of Hispaniola with Haiti, Spanish is the main language used in daily life. The climate is mild enough in winter for beach resorts to attract visitors from the United States, and baseball is the king of sports.

Home to approximately 10 million people, the Dominican is a former colony of Spain, and it was first "discovered" as part of the New World on Christopher Columbus's 1492 voyage. He reached landfall on December 5 of that year on the first of his four sailing missions to the Americas.

In 1496, Columbus' brother Bartholomew built Santo Domingo, the city that remains the capital of the country to this day and has a population of about 3 million.

Today, Juan Marichal and his family live in a spacious, fenced-in home in the heart of the city.

Spain ruled the Dominican Republic for 300 years, but there was also intermittent occupation by Haiti, France, and the United States. Rafael Trujillo emerged as dictator in the early 1930s and ruled with an iron fist until his assassination in 1961. The Trujillo family exerted control over the early aspects of Marichal's baseball career.

Baseball is by far the most popular sport on the island. Its origins date back more than 100 years, when the game was introduced by Cubans—not, as some people have contended, by the U.S. military. While otherwise keeping busy running the nation, Trujillo was a passionate fan, and he is at the center of a famous baseball story from the 1930s. Determined to capture the national baseball title with a team representing his government, Trujillo sent an emissary to the United States to lure legendary pitcher Satchel Paige and his handpicked team to play a season for the leader.

Paige, the Negro Leagues' biggest star, was known not only for his skill but for his willingness to travel anywhere for a payday. He was given money to put together a team, and he rounded up a good one, including outfielder Cool Papa Bell, reputed to be the fastest man ever to play the game.

Paige and his squad went into the final game of the championship series tied with the upstart team that Trujillo so badly wanted to beat. Paige later reported that the Americans were thrown into a jail overnight before the last game and feared they would be shot if they didn't win.

They won and fled the island, Paige said. It was never clear how much Paige exaggerated details of the story, but he retold it many times.

The story took hold and may have scared off some American ballplayers for a time. But even more significant to Dominican fans, the attempt by Trujillo and others to buy a title backfired economically and bankrupted the league. It took several years, into the mid-1950s, before the six-team Dominican winter league was reformed and regained its equilibrium. There are still six teams in the league; Escogido is Marichal's favorite and the one he pitched for when he came home from summer play in the United States.

Marichal was obsessed with baseball as a young boy, and he occasionally got in trouble with his mother for skipping school to play his beloved sport. They lived in a wood-frame house at the edge of the large family farm. The house was big enough to hold three bedrooms—one for Marichal's mother, Natividad; one for his sister, Maria; and one for Juan and his two older brothers, Gonzalo and Rafael, to share. The house's thatched roof consisted of banana leaves, and sometimes during the rainy season the water seeped in. Gonzalo and Rafael generally took turns making the repairs.

There was no electricity and thus no radio or television. And there was no money for baseball equipment. To play the game he loved, Marichal and his friends made their own baseballs, bats, and gloves. They made do with what they had.

While playing for the local team in Laguna Verde, Marichal caught the attention of the Trujillo family, who enlisted him into the Air Force to play baseball when he was still a teenager. Although Marichal never got to realize his dream of learning to fly airplanes, the young pitcher traveled throughout Latin America with the Air Force team, eventually exposing him to the inquisitive eyes of scouts from the American major leagues.

From poor beginnings, it was a long road for Marichal to reach the status of national icon and baseball Hall of Famer.

MY FATHER, FRANCISCO, CAME FROM THE CANARY ISLANDS IN SPAIN. MY MOTHER, NATIVIDAD, IS FROM A TOWN NEAR Santiago, the second-largest city in the Dominican Republic. It is a beautiful place. They are nice people there. My mother was a beautiful woman. She grew up with her mother and father and she was one of nine brothers and sisters. I had lots of aunts and uncles.

My father came to the Dominican Republic from Spain at a very young age. His family was a big family, too. Marichal is only one family in the Dominican Republic. Whoever has that name is related to me. My mother's side is Sanchez. There are many, many people named Sanchez here, but most of them are not related to me.

My parents were living in a town called Gurabo, near Santiago, and they decided to move west, to an area very close to Haiti. That's how we got to Laguna Verde. My hometown is 50 miles from the border. There are beautiful mountains there, but we lived in a flatter area and had a farm.

This whole area is farming. Everyone grows lots of rice, plantain, bananas, beans, corn, yucca, and sweet potato—a lot of different crops. My grandmother and her husband on my mother's side moved to Monte Cristi, near Laguna Verde, and got land in that area. I was born on a farm and I worked on a farm from the time I was a little boy.

My father died very young. I was three years old. I didn't know that he had an illness. Nobody knew. Nobody knows what he died from. I don't remember him and feel like I never really met him.

I have one older sister, Maria Altagracia, and two brothers, Gonzalo and Rafael. I am the youngest. Gonzalo is six years older than me and Rafael is four years older. My sister is the oldest, nine years older than me.

Most people called me Juan, but one of my aunts gave me a nickname. She called me "Manico." I don't know why she did, or what it means. Later, Horace Stoneham, the owner of the Giants, called me "Juanito." He liked me very much, and it was a sign of affection.

On the farm, we had all the food we needed. The only thing we had to bring in was salt, and oil from a pig, because in those days you didn't cook with olive oil. In my house there was no money, but lots of food. We didn't even have electricity. We lit the house with gas lamps and we had an outhouse, or *letrina*, for a bathroom.

At the end of every day, even when I skipped school to play baseball, I had to do chores on the farm. I took care of the horses and a donkey. At one point we had close to 500 head of goat. Rafael and I were in charge of those animals. We had to bring the grass for them to eat, and we had to go into the mountains to bring the goats back to the corral every day. That took us a long time. Sometimes we did not get back to the house until 10:30 or 11 at night. We worked very hard on that farm.

I loved living on a farm, and I also loved baseball. My older brother Gonzalo taught me all about baseball and pitching. Let me tell you, Gonzalo was a good ballplayer. He was awesome. He was so good that he could play every position. During one game when the catcher got hurt, I saw him come in from right field to put on the catching gear and get behind the plate. The feeling I got watching that was something special. I was so proud I got goose bumps. He could do anything on the baseball field. He was that good.

My brother Rafael didn't like baseball. We played all the time in the neighborhood, and he never played. He just wasn't interested. My sister, Maria, didn't play, either.

When Gonzalo played, I tagged along with him. I loved to watch him pitch. He helped me with my pitching, and with my batting and fielding, too. That's how I learned. He was so good that when the team from our hometown wasn't playing, he sometimes was invited to play for other teams. He was not a professional, though. They did not pay him. He loved the game so much. Today, if you had a player of his caliber, teams would have to pay him $5 million or $6 million to play for them. Many scouts from all over would be after him.

One of my uncles owned a *tienda*, a store where they sold clothes, food—something like a department store—and Gonzalo worked for my uncle. He spent most of his time at the store in Monte Cristi. I went to school, but on Sundays I got on a horse, rode to Monte Cristi, and picked Gonzalo up and brought him home. Riding the horse from Laguna Verde took about an hour. Then I took him back that night.

I did more horseback riding than John Wayne, but I was in love with that brother. Gonzalo was my idol and my teacher. He helped me so much. He kept pitching until he was about 20, but then he left the store and began working for a company that built windmills.

Gonzalo was very good-looking and he liked to go out with girls. Sometimes he would rather go out with a girl instead of going to play baseball. I think he was only 21 when he got married. That's been known to happen with girls. But he was so good.

Whenever I wasn't working on the farm, I tried to play baseball. We always played baseball on Saturday and Sunday and whenever we could sneak away from school. Weekdays we'd leave home at about eight o'clock in the morning to go to school, and sometimes we never made it. I stopped with other kids to play baseball. But then the teacher came to the house to tell my mother and she was not happy.

She would say to me—many times—"My son, what are you going to do when you grow up if you don't have an education?"

From the time I was six or seven years old, I was telling my mother I was going to be a baseball player.

All my friends were like me. They lived on farms and had no money to buy baseball equipment. We found golf balls, but of course they were too small to use, so we used cloth and rolled that around the ball to make it the size of a baseball. Between us, we found one peso and brought this ball to the shoemaker and paid him to make a covering.

For bats we used branches from a *wassama*. That kind of tree held lots of water so when we got a branch that was the right size, we would lay it down in the sun to dry. After it dried out it was really lightweight and made a good bat. But because it was so light it didn't always last very long before breaking.

Then we had to make gloves. We got material like the tarp that is used on the top of a truck. We put our hand out on the cloth, took out a pencil, and drew around it, and then we cut the tarp into gloves. That's how we used to play. There was not much padding.

We didn't have much choice, since we never had money to buy equipment. A lot of players throughout Latin America had to do this in order to play—in other countries, too, not just the Dominican. We just love the game so much that, as a kid, anywhere you had a chance to play, anywhere you saw other kids playing, you wanted to be there.

In those days even girls liked to play baseball with the boys. The Alou brothers have a sister named Zula, and they told me she was much better than Matty and Jesus. They said she used to play good ball, and considering that Felipe, Matty, and Jesus all played in the majors, she must have been pretty good.

My mother did not think my career choice was a very smart one. She would say, "What are you going to do except play baseball? How are you going to support your family when you get married?" I told her, "Mother, you're going to be so proud when you hear my name on the radio."

I didn't even know that I could make money playing baseball. She didn't, either. At that time there were no major league players from the Dominican Republic. The first Dominican in the majors was Ozzie Virgil Sr., who broke in with the New York Giants in 1956. Ozzie was from Monte Cristi, and there is an airport named after him in the Dominican.

I kept telling my mother she would hear my name on the radio and her friends would hear it and they would come up to her and she would say, "Oh, that's my Manico, my son." We used to have arguments all the time about my playing baseball, especially if I missed school. She was okay with me playing baseball as long as I didn't stay out of school. That she didn't agree with.

But I was a good player. During the summer of 1954 I spent time in Santo Domingo with my brother Gonzalo, and I could play baseball during that whole time off from school. Gonzalo took me to see my first baseball game in Santo Domingo. I was so close to those baseball players that I thought they were gods.

From that time on I learned what it was to be a little boy to look up to baseball players, and when I was a baseball player I tried to please everyone because I remembered what it was like as a little kid.

I remember a guy named Willard Brown, a black guy from the United States who was the first guy I got close to and looked up to. Alonzo Perry was a big star in Mexico and the Dominican, and he led the Dominican in home runs twice. What a hitter. I started watching him as a kid and I ended up playing in his era for a year or two before he retired. I think I pitched to him once and I think I got him out, but I was a rookie and getting that man out even late in his career was tough. I followed that man for years.

When I was a kid, first I was a fan of the team from Aguilas. And when I saw the Olivo brothers pitch, Diomedes and Chi-Chi, I hated them because they played for another team. Later, when I became a professional, we became friends. I told them I hated them when I was a kid. They laughed and said, "I don't blame you." The day Diomedes died I went to the funeral and I leaned on the coffin and I thought my heart was going to come out.

Baseball was always popular in the Dominican Republic. It was always No. 1 compared to other sports. Soccer is the biggest sport in some Latin American countries, but we don't care so much about soccer. Soccer is maybe No. 3. I started playing baseball at six or seven years old, but we never played soccer when I was a kid. Baseball was always the biggest thing.

We once had a terrible tragedy with the national team. On January 11, 1948, the whole team, the best players from the Dominican, were killed in a plane crash, except for one player who didn't make the trip. The country worked to rebuild the team. When I was a kid, one of the reasons I wanted to be a baseball player was because I wanted to be a member of the national team. That was my ambition, to be a member of that team. I didn't know anything about any other teams and I did not even think about the major leagues.

There was summer league baseball back then, but the winter league did not start until 1955. A lot of the black players from the Negro Leagues in the United States played in the Dominican Republic. They were not given fair chances in the United States because of discrimination, but they were welcome here in the Dominican. Oh yes, Satchel Paige, Cool Papa Bell, Josh Gibson, Buck Leonard, they came, and Orlando Cepeda's father, Perucho, he played too. I have a photo of a 1937 team with a lot of those guys.

The first team that I played for was Las Flores in Monte Cristi. I did not always want to be a pitcher. My first position was shortstop. I was a very good hitter, and I loved to play every day. I loved to hit. But I got a chance to see a game with the new national team and I watched Bombo Ramos pitch. He made such an impression on me.

Bombo Ramos was so good that he sometimes told batters, "I'm going to strike you out." And he did it! It was funny to hear. He would tell them, "I'm going to throw a fastball. You better hit it." He threw so fast, nobody could touch it. After the batter missed, Ramos would say, "Oh, you didn't hit it. You're not going to hit this one. You're not going to hit the next one." The batters got mad, they got frustrated.

That guy became my idol because of the way he pitched. They didn't have radar guns then, but I think Ramos used to throw 100-mph fastballs. When I went back to Laguna Verde, I told my brothers and all my friends that I wasn't going to play shortstop anymore. I told them I was going to be a pitcher like Bombo Ramos.

The only thing I did the rest of that summer was throw like Bombo Ramos. He threw sidearm and I wanted to throw just like him, so I threw sidearm.

A baseball fan who knew me in San Francisco would not have recognized me pitching back then—and even after I first went to the minor leagues in the United States. For a couple of years after I first saw Ramos pitch, I threw sidearm. It was a while before anyone asked me why I threw that way.

"That's how I learned," I said. This was a coach and he asked me if I had ever had a sore arm and I said no, I hadn't. I hadn't wanted to go through the whole Bombo Ramos story, but I realized I had better. I explained about how he was my idol and everything. The coach looked at me and said I probably should learn how to throw overhand. But for a while I was a full-time sidearmer.

Although we did not have much money, I remember my childhood as being like a dream. I was happy on the farm and I loved baseball. We lived near Rio Yaque del Norte, the biggest river in the Dominican Republic. It goes right past our land, my mother's farm at that time, and let me tell you, we used to have so much fun swimming in that river. I fished, too.

One Sunday we would go fishing and the next Sunday we would go hunting with a slingshot. I was very good at that. I know there are all these stories about boys with slingshots and how they broke windows, but in my neighborhood I don't think we had a house with a glass window at that time. So there was no way you could break one. I was very good at hitting birds with rocks and knocking them down.

I didn't have a father around, but I had never known him. My mother is the reason we grew up so happy. That lady was so strong, and after I grew up and had kids I realized why she was so strong. She wanted us to be perfect. She didn't want us to do anything wrong. She really wanted us to be good people when we grew up. That's how she was raising us.

My mother was very strict and I didn't always like that when I was a kid, but now I'm very happy she raised us that way. My mother worried about us a lot. She always worried that something would happen to us in the river.

One thing that was done in my neighborhood was a communal workday. People would come from all over the community to work for one day on the farm. My mother would cook for everybody. We would get a bull and cook that, maybe three or four goats, rice, beans, everything. The people would not get paid for helping us, but they got a great meal. She told all the people who came to help that they could bring their kids, too.

The way it worked was that all the kids got called over first and ate, and then all the adults ate. On one communal workday when I was 10 years old, we were working on separating the weeds from the grass and the rice plants. That was the job of the day. To do that right you have to irrigate every square inch with water about a foot or two feet deep. We ate between noon and one o'clock, and after we ate, the kids all ran off back to the river.

It was not to go swimming, as I so often did. We were just fooling around. I remember that I was next to my grandmother. We used to call her Vieja and suddenly I said, "Vieja, I'm dreaming." I remember exactly what happened. I said, "I'm dreaming," and she said, "What are you dreaming of?" I said, "I'm dreaming that I'm digging gold from the ground."

And then I fell over, just like that, into the water. I don't remember what happened after that. People rushed over to help pull me out of the water. The whole event broke up. My family got me onto a horse—I was unconscious and they told me all this later—and brought me into the house.

When I was at the house, someone got a car and took me to a clinic at Monte Cristi. Someone had called the doctor there ahead of time. When I got to the clinic I was still unconscious, and they put me to bed. I did not regain consciousness for nine days.

It was explained to me that I had something where my eating and then jumping around caused some kind of food indigestion. In Spanish they call it *mala digestion*—bad digestion. It was unusual, and no matter what they did at the clinic, I did not regain consciousness. My family was very frightened.

The doctors decided they could do nothing more for me at the clinic, and a doctor told one of my uncles that the family should take me home. He told my uncle that when I got home I should be given baths in real, real hot water, that it would be good for the human body to absorb all of that steam. So my family took me home and began giving me those baths. The doctor did not have too much faith that I would survive.

I think that's why he told my family to take me home. So my uncles went to work when we got home, boiling water—well not quite boiling, but making up pots of very hot water. They did this for a few days and the steam was all over the place. One night they started doing the baths at eight o'clock, and at midnight I woke up.

According to a story told in my family, the doctor said to my relatives that if I didn't wake up by midnight that night I would die. My family said that at quarter to twelve, words came out of my mouth, and that was the first indication I was going to be okay. But it may have been just sleep talking. No one has ever really understood this part.

About a year or two before I went into the coma, I was sleepwalking in my house. I actually sleepwalked playing baseball. I ran from one room to another playing baseball with a man I didn't know. This man was not much older than me and I was really playing baseball with him, it felt. I was moving from room to room and saying, "Throw it. Throw me the ball." In the middle of the night I was doing that. I thought it was because I would go to bed thinking so much about the game, I played baseball in my dreams. It was good exercise, right?

After I woke up from my coma, little by little, I got better, but I was still weak. I had been in a coma for nine days. I didn't know what was happening because I was unconscious, but afterward I was a little bit scared.

Except for that experience, I don't think I would mind going back to live my childhood again. It was so beautiful that I wouldn't mind.

We were very religious in my family, a Catholic family, and I often wear religious medallions. The family church was very beautiful.

To get to this church we had to pass a river, and after church my friends and I used to swim in the river. I would often go with Felipe and Matty Alou and another friend named Chichi Garcia, who also played baseball. Chichi went to the United States, too, and played in the minors, but he did not make it to the majors.

As I was growing up I kept playing baseball with my friends, and once I became a pitcher I was good enough to get noticed by the local team. In 1956, I was contacted to play for the Grenada Company, which was part of the United Fruit Company. They were very big in Latin America. They approached my mother and asked her for permission to let me play and told her I would make $18 a week.

When United Fruit Company was around, it had the richest team in the Dominican Republic. In my hometown, in that area, they were everything. They recruited me to play baseball, so I left high school and went to work for them. I was given a place to live and expected to play baseball on weekends.

They put me and other players on the payroll just to play baseball. They paid us pretty well, but we made more money when they had a shipment of bananas going out of a port city and the company sent us over there. It took three or four days for the bananas to be loaded into the big ships, and the people that ran the company and the team wanted us to make some extra money.

The hard work was loading the bananas. We were the inspectors, which was the easy work, and we didn't know anything about bananas. They just put us there to collect extra money. We went through the motions. For three days we did that and we made good money for that time. They did it because they liked us as baseball players and wanted to keep us happy and playing for the team.

There were things even the United Fruit Company couldn't control, however. Our team was good and we won our area championship on the western side of the Dominican Republic. So we advanced to the national championships. We went up against the Dominican Air Force team in the championship, and I pitched. I pitched a good game and beat that team 2–1. I was just about 18 years old, so I was young and had good potential.

I liked playing for the United Fruit Company. I knew all the players from our area. I was still living at home, and I was happy with the way things were going. I was playing baseball and getting paid to do it, one way or the other.

I beat the Air Force team on a Sunday morning, and after our games were over we went back to the house the team was staying in. It was a beautiful location, right on the water. We could swim in the ocean and it was pretty good living. The next morning at eight o'clock, somebody knocked on the door. It was a lieutenant in the Air Force holding a telegram—for me.

The commander in chief of the Air Force team was Ramfis Trujillo, General Trujillo's son. The officer was delivering a telegram from Ramfis saying that I was to report right away to join the Air Force, and his signature was on it. I was a little bit shaky when I saw that. This really meant it was an order from Ramfis' father, the man who ran the country. In our country at this time, if such a document was presented to you, it was considered to be "an order from God." I was still a teenager and I had no plans to join the Air Force. I just wanted to play baseball.

The officer left the telegram with me. I took a shower at the house, got all of my clothes and baseball equipment together, and went to my hometown as fast as I could. I immediately showed the telegram to my mother, and she didn't like it. She said that a kid just 18 years old should not join the Air Force, that I was too young. She started pacing back and forth in the house.

She was trying to come up with an idea to keep me out of the Air Force, but she did not say anything. About four o'clock that afternoon, the same lieutenant showed up at our farm with another telegram that said the same thing. When my mother saw the second telegram she said, "Son, you cannot say no to those people." I was waiting for her to make a decision on what I should do, but by then I think I knew what it would be. You did not disobey an order from God. By then I was prepared to go because I knew I had no choice. We knew the reputation of the type of people we were dealing with. They got what they wanted. If they wanted me to play baseball for the Air Force team, I had to play for that team.

At about six o'clock the next morning I left home to join the Air Force. I reported to an office to sign in and "volunteer" in front of a general. I told him that I loved airplanes and I wanted to go to school to learn how to fly them. He said, "Oh, you're going to have a chance to go to school here and play baseball." After I signed in, it was nothing but baseball. No school. I actually did want to fly planes. I thought I'd love it.

This was all a big irony. At Laguna Verde all I wanted to do was play baseball and I didn't care about going to school. Now that I wanted to take advantage of going to school to fly planes, all they wanted me to do was play baseball.

From the first moment I signed up for the Air Force, I was welcomed. Before I left his office, the general who signed me into the service opened up his wallet, pulled out a 100-peso note, and gave it to me. It was the first time I had ever seen 100 pesos. I had seen 10, 20, and 50 pesos, but 100 pesos I never saw before.

He wanted me to use the money to eat from the officers' restaurant that day. So I ate with the 100 pesos. After that I had to get used to the other food that was for all the men. I had to get used to food that was not as good.

My job in the Air Force was to pitch every week. In 14 months in the Air Force I lost three games. I had been forced to switch teams to play for the Air Force, but once I started playing there I loved it. We traveled to Puerto Rico to play. We went to Aruba. We went to Mexico. I got to see and play in a lot of places.

I even got used to the discipline. It was good for me. To this day I tell myself that I'm very happy that happened.

One very strange thing that happened to us when I was in the Air Force was when the team got sent to jail for losing. We played against

Manzanillo in a doubleheader one Sunday morning and afternoon. We lost both games, and when we got back to the capital the general wanted to know why we lost both games. We told him the whole story. They were close games. It was really just that the other guys played better that day. One reason was that most of our players got sick because of the water. He didn't believe that story, so they sent a commission to Manzanillo to investigate. In the meantime they kept the whole team in jail, including the manager, who was an Air Force captain. He got 30 days. Other than that I didn't have complaints about the Air Force.

It may sound funny, but I think one of the things that helped me quite a bit to make the major leagues was going into the Air Force. I didn't want to go and I only joined because they made me, but I believe the best thing that happened to me as a person was being in the Air Force.

I was not really part of the Air Force the way most people would think. Even if I wanted to fly planes, the only thing they had me do was pitch. I played baseball morning, afternoon, and night, the way I always wanted to do when I had skipped school as a kid. We played games all over the Caribbean, sometimes in Puerto Rico, sometimes in Venezuela. We used to travel to Mexico.

Some of the kids I grew up with never left the farm, never left our hometown. Some have passed away. I could have been just another farmer.

Some of these friends played baseball, but they weren't attractive enough to scouts the way I was. Playing for the Air Force team got me noticed. I was seen by a lot more people at the championships in other countries than would have seen me if I had just been playing in the Dominican Republic. If I hadn't entered the Air Force, nobody would have known about me.

Another thing that really helped me in the Air Force was the discipline. In the morning you had to be dressed and ready by eight o'clock. Then we had to clean the barracks. We had to pick up every little piece of paper or anything that doesn't belong there, wash the dishes and dry them.

Once we dressed, ate, and cleaned everything, we took a bus to the baseball field. At noon we came back and picked up our food, and then we returned to the stadium and ate it in the bleachers. Then we lay down and rested for an hour or so, and at 2 P.M. we played baseball again. There was nothing but baseball for us.

We had the best team in the country and we wanted to win. Once in a while Trujillo showed up to watch us. I was lucky because every time he showed up to see a game and I was pitching, I pitched well. I didn't know when he was coming, but I never got nervous, even though he sat right behind home plate.

At that time there were not many scouts from the majors in Latin America, only about four or five teams. If I had been living in the country instead of pitching for the Air Force in Santo Domingo, they never would have seen me.

CHAPTER 3

A New-Look Juan
in a New Home

*A*lthough Juan Marichal never got closer to piloting a
plane than the average frequent-flyer air traveler, his
time in the Dominican Air Force proved to be a fruitful
experience. He developed as a pitcher, and his prominent
role with one of the top teams in his country led to his
discovery by scouts from the United States.

Marichal stayed focused on baseball while in the Air
Force and worked very hard at his pitching, fine-tuning what
had always been pinpoint control. It was his throwing accuracy
more than the speed of his fastball that brought Marichal
results and gained him the attention of major league teams.

Given the power wielded by the Trujillo family,
including over the lives of its baseball players, it would

not have been unusual for the Trujillos to have prevented Marichal from moving on to the top professional ranks in the world. However, when teams did come to inquire about Marichal's services, Ramfis Trujillo did not refuse, did not bargain hard, and only at first placed minimal restrictions on his departure. Once he was old enough, Marichal was able to sign with the San Francisco Giants and go to the United States to play baseball.

He signed with the Giants organization in 1958 and began a journey through the minors to such places as Michigan City, Indiana; Springfield, Massachusetts; and Tacoma, Washington, before he got his call up to the majors in July 1960.

Upon arriving in the United States in the late 1950s, Marichal discovered there a side of life for which he was not completely prepared. His new country was steeped in racism. In many parts of the country, a man with dark skin like his own could expect to be treated rudely or unfairly, or be outright discriminated against. It was not so easy to get along, either, if you didn't speak the language. Marichal was young and inexperienced in life, had limited knowledge of English, and was a man in a dark-skinned body. None of that made adjusting to a new land an easy proposition.

Neither did having to learn how to pitch all over again. The man who would come to have the most distinctive high-kick delivery of any pitcher in history was solely a sidearm thrower when he arrived in the States. Marichal was two years into his minor league career before his style evolved into the one for which he became famous.

When Richie Klaus, manager of the Giants' Class C team in St. Cloud, Minnesota, first saw Marichal pitching sidearm during spring training in Sanford, Florida, in 1958, he predicted that Marichal would hurt his arm throwing that way and said he would have to change his form. At the same time, Klaus admired Marichal's abilities and was happy to turn him over to the manager of the Class D Michigan City club, Buddy Kerr, a man who would be a great influence on the young pitcher.

Perfecting his new overhand style, Marichal soon worked his way up through the Giants' farm system. He posted impressive numbers at Class A Springfield in 1959, winning 18 games with a sparkling 2.39 earned run average and 208 strikeouts in 271 innings. He was a workhorse, completing 23 of his 37 starts.

He performed well at spring training in 1960, but Marichal, who suffered a number of injuries during his career, had some bad luck on the mound. A line drive back to the box during batting practice hit him flush below the belt (it was announced for public consumption that he was hit in the abdomen), knocking him to the ground.

The pain was excruciating, and Marichal was taken to a nearby hospital. He was laid up for nearly a week.

Giants manager Bill Rigney asked Marichal when he would be able to pitch. As eager as he was to show off his talents, the young hopeful had to admit that he didn't know. His recovery lagged, and the next time the manager encountered Marichal he told the pitcher he was being farmed out to the AAA Tacoma affiliate in the Pacific Coast League.

Still, Rigney spoke favorably of Marichal's skills and informed him that when he showed his stuff in Tacoma, he would surely be brought up to the big-league club.

Marichal was disappointed not to be making the trip to San Francisco, but he also believed it would not be long before he was pitching for the Giants. By mid-May, Marichal regained his top form and would soon prove himself worthy of major league consideration.

IN THE 1950S, MAJOR LEAGUE TEAMS WERE ONLY JUST BEGINNING TO SCOUT LATIN AMERICAN COUNTRIES AND SIGN Latin ballplayers. Only a few teams were checking it out at first. The Washington Senators, the Pittsburgh Pirates, the San Francisco Giants, and the Los Angeles Dodgers were the pioneers in looking for players in Latin America.

Camilo Pascual, from Cuba, was pitching for the Washington Senators and he saw me when I was playing for the Air Force. He came and told me, "Don't sign with anybody. Don't see anybody." He wanted the Senators to sign me. But it was a good thing I didn't listen to him because if I waited for that guy from the Senators, I might still be waiting at my house. He never showed up.

One scout saw me strike out 18 batters in a game, and the Yankees said they were interested in me. At that point in time the Yankees were not known for signing Latin players. But this guy seemed to have an agreement with them, and every time I pitched he was right there watching. So he knew about me.

This guy told me he was going to sign me and he went to Ramfis Trujillo. Ramfis told him he should take Pedro Gonzalez, too. Gonzalez was a very good ballplayer, but he was a second baseman and the Yankees already had Bobby Richardson. They signed Pedro and they wanted to leave me in the Air Force for another year, and then bring me to the United States after that. I think it was because I was so young. But when they came back to sign me, Ramfis said no. He wanted me to pitch for Escogido.

I did pitch for Escogido—they were always my team in the Dominican. That's where the Giants saw me. The Giants had a better record with Latin players than the Yankees, anyway, and my friend Felipe Alou was already with them. I was always happy that I became a Giant. I tell everybody that I left my heart in San Francisco.

The Giants did not give me much money to sign—$500. It was not a lot, but I was so happy when they told me I was going to be signed and go to the United States to play baseball. I reminded myself that I had promised my mother that I was going to become a professional baseball player, and this was it.

As a kid I did not follow the majors. My only ambition was to play for the Dominican national team, but I knew this was bigger. The man who signed me for the Giants was Horacio Martinez, who was an ex-ballplayer. He had played in the Negro Leagues, and he told me a little bit about what to expect, but I had to live it for myself.

When I was growing up in the Dominican Republic there was never any racism. Everyone was the same. It didn't matter what the color of your skin was. We never thought about it.

When I signed with the Giants in 1958, the minor leaguers and the major leaguers all went to the same spring training camp. The team headquarters was in Sanford, Florida. Some of us, I don't know how we survived. When I went to Sanford for the first time, I found out it was a very racist town. I was most shocked to see different groups treated different ways, how everyone split up, whites, blacks, Latins. I started asking questions because I didn't even know about racism.

People started telling me right away that, in the United States, Latins and blacks couldn't get together with a white girl for a date. I said to myself, "Here I am in the biggest country in the world with that kind of prejudice." It was unbelievable, terrible.

I was young and excited and this was a big opportunity, and then I was confronted by all this racism. It got very discouraging at times.

When training camp broke up, the Giants split up all the players in the organization. The major leaguers went to San Francisco, of course. The minor leaguers were sent to different towns.

I was assigned to Michigan City, Indiana, and we were traveling by bus from Sanford. I did not know where Michigan City was. I had never heard of it. Michigan City was in the Class D league. The Giants were starting me out at the bottom.

The Giants were a progressive team at that time. I was not the only Latin or dark-skinned player on that bus. There were seven of us, three Latins and four blacks. The ride north was going to take three days. The roads were not as good as they are now and the bus was slow. We had to stop to eat. The first time we stopped, we were still in the South. The seven of us could not get off the bus to eat. There was a guy with us, a Cuban merchant from Key West, who was our translator. He spoke English and Spanish and he went in to get our food.

Our manager, Buddy Kerr, felt very badly about this. That man, I will never forget. He was like a father to us. He was such a kind person. He made sure that we had something to eat before he ate. He showed that he cared about us. Any time I see somebody like that who doesn't care about the color of your skin, he is going to be my friend forever. You can't judge people by race or color. You judge people by their actions, how they behave. I love that man because he was good to us all the time. He was there for us. One of the reasons we survived this prejudice was because of Buddy Kerr.

It was very hard to believe this was the United States. It was such a shock for me. I can't say I got angry, but it was sad.

I don't want to be negative. I always want to be positive. That is part of my philosophy. But I couldn't be positive about the racism in the United States. I was very homesick at the time, too, and that just made it worse.

When I left the Dominican Republic I brought a lot of records with me. Those were the old 78 rpms and we had a record player. I loved the music. All of the Latin players listened to it. We got together every night. But after a little while it got too hard. The music was supposed to help me, but it made me more homesick. There was a story that I broke all the records on purpose, but I didn't. I gave them away. I told the other guys, "Don't invite me to listen anymore." I just told them I couldn't take it.

There were times I was so homesick that I wanted to go back and be with my family on the farm in Laguna Verde. But I always remembered what I had promised my mother about becoming a success in baseball. That was a motivator for me. She had to hear my name on the radio. She also did not have very much money, and I knew that I could help her more from the United States than I could if I went back. All those thoughts came up in my mind, and I thank God that He gave me the power to overcome all of that and stay in the United States.

I saw friends leave and go back to the Dominican. Some left for a couple of days and came back to the States. Some left for good.

When you are in the clubhouse with all the players and a music box playing and all your teammates are around, that's a feeling of being together. But when you go to a strange city and everyone goes his own way—at night, especially—that's when you feel homesickness most.

When I came to the United States my English was not very good at all. I didn't even know how to ask for a glass of water. I was lucky that on every team I played for, there was some player from another

Latin American country or someone around who spoke Spanish who could help me. But not speaking English was an extra hardship. It was really, really hard for me.

I have seen so many changes since those days. Back then if you grew up in the Dominican Republic, you didn't learn to speak English, especially if you lived on a farm in the country like I did. Now more young players learn English. And we were such strangers in the United States. In the 1950s and 1960s, Americans didn't learn to speak Spanish. Now there are so many Latin American people in the United States and so many people speak Spanish. I did not think I would ever see that.

We spent a lot of time on that bus heading north from Florida. They even changed drivers during the trip. Every time we stopped to refuel you would see the white guys on the team going in the front door of the restaurant, and we had to wait to find out if we had to eat on the bus or if the restaurant was going to let us eat at the kitchen in back.

This was an insult to us, too. I always think that all human beings are the same. We should all be treated like human beings. Why does this happen? Being in Sanford and on this bus ride were not the only times that I experienced racism during my baseball career.

Later, when I was with the Giants, we were in Houston playing the Colt .45s. The movie *Cleopatra* was playing, starring Elizabeth Taylor and Richard Burton. Orlando Cepeda wanted to go see the movie and he wanted me to come with him. I said I would not go.

"Orlando," I said, "We are in Texas. We are in Houston. The reality is, they won't let us in." I adapt to the circumstances. Orlando said, "So, you don't want to go. I'm going." I said, "Good luck." He left and about 45 minutes later somebody knocked on the door. I thought it was the maid coming to clean the room. I opened the door and saw Orlando. I couldn't stop laughing when I saw his face, although it was not really funny. They would not sell him a ticket. It was the South.

In those days with the Giants, we were given two tickets to every game if we wanted to leave them for guests, home and away. You just told the traveling secretary if you wanted to use them. In some cities players knew a lot of people and I didn't know anyone, so I gave them my tickets to use. When I needed tickets I asked the guys and they gave me theirs if they didn't need them. That's how the whole thing worked.

One time some other guy from the team came up to us and said, "You can't leave a ticket for a white girl." He didn't even know us. We were leaving tickets for Mexican girls. Another time I called a house to talk to a girl and no one spoke Spanish. I was told later I had to speak English.

When we first came to the United States with the Giants, the team had Alex Pompez speak with us. He was an official with the Negro Leagues and then became a big scout for the Giants. He made it to the Hall of Fame. But they had him talk to us in Spanish, not about baseball but about what behavior was expected from us. He told us what to do and what not to do, especially in public.

When we finally got to Michigan City after the long bus ride, the team had arranged for three guys to live with a black family. The white guys were in a hotel. I had to stay with a black family because my skin is light brown. I am not white and I am not black, but I count as dark.

The family was very nice and it was wonderful being with them. We became good friends. They loved us. We had a great, great friendship with that family. They were very good to us and we had fun with them, but what was wrong is that we didn't have a choice where to stay. In the minors we were just teammates in the clubhouse, on the field, and on the bus.

We never had any problems with the fans in Michigan City. I never heard names being called or anything bad there. When we went on the road, there was some name-calling. Maybe it was because we were the opposite team. But it wasn't too bad.

I played in Michigan City for one year. Buddy Kerr treated us very well, treated us all like human beings. He also taught me a lot about baseball. He had been a major league player and a good player. He was a shortstop during the 1940s and early 1950s, most of his career with the New York Giants. I was not even 19 years old yet, and I knew that I didn't know everything. I understood that baseball is a game that, no matter how old you are or how much you have seen it, if you watch it every day you will learn something new.

I knew I had a lot to learn, and I wanted to learn. I was still throwing nothing but sidearm in Michigan City. I had a sidearm fastball and a sidearm curve from the right to the left. That's all.

I pitched 245 innings as a rookie in Michigan City, and I struck out 246 batters. I was very confident when I had two strikes on a batter. I was better throwing sidearm against right-handed hitters because they didn't like to see the ball coming at them that way, from behind them and across the plate. I won 21 games and then two more in the playoffs. One man who was a butcher was such a big fan of mine that every time I won a game he gave me a chicken. It was a good thing I loved to eat chicken.

The next year the Giants sent me to Springfield, Massachusetts, which was Class A, and the manager was Andy Gilbert. I was throwing sidearm there, too, right up until the last two weeks of the season.

Finally, Andy asked me, "Why do you throw like that?" I told him about Bombo Ramos, the Dominican pitcher I had admired when I was younger. He asked me, "Do you want to learn how to throw overhand?" I was doing very well and I didn't want to take a risk about my future, so I asked him what would be the difference if I changed my delivery. He said, "You will be a much, much better pitcher against left-handed hitters." When he told me that, I agreed that I should learn. I thought it was time to learn to throw all ways, not just sidearm.

Right away I went to the bullpen and started throwing to a catcher. I had no mechanics to throw overhand. They didn't even use that word—*mechanics*—back then. I needed new form. I was told to raise my arm and bring my elbow over my shoulder and then release the ball from there. It seemed that I couldn't do it without lifting up my leg. High kicking with my front leg started that day.

Although I started practicing throwing overhand while I was with Springfield and kept it up for the last couple of weeks of the season, I never used that motion in a game. It was too soon. I only had one more start the rest of the season, anyway. I had to make the change through repetition, but I fell in love with the style and saw that I could throw more pitches and thought I would be more effective, so it wasn't that hard. I felt like I was throwing a little bit harder with the same control. That's why I liked it so much right away.

I was invited to spring training with the major league team before the 1960 season, but I don't think the Giants were counting on me that year. They invited me without a contract. If they thought I was going to make the team they would have put me on the 40-man roster.

It turned out to be the worst spring training. They told me they wanted me to pitch batting practice every day. I think that was to help me get used to throwing with my new overhand style. We were in Arizona, but it was cold and I don't like cold weather.

When I got to Phoenix I was pitching every day, but that wasn't the real problem. I developed a really bad rash in my groin area from my athletic supporter. It was so bad that the skin was coming off and I was bleeding. The pitching coach, Larry Jansen, told me they were going to give me a day off the next day. I was glad. I said to myself, "Good, I don't think I can pitch this way." That day, since I wasn't going to pitch, I didn't put on my athletic supporter with the cup.

I went out to the outfield to catch fly balls. A few minutes later a coach came to tell me they had changed their mind and they wanted me on the pitching mound. I was a rookie and I was too afraid to tell him to wait while I ran into the clubhouse to put on my athletic supporter. So I went to the mound with no support. This was before they would put pitching screens in front of the mound to protect the batting practice pitcher.

The first batter, on the first pitch, hit a line drive right at me and hit me in the right testicle. I cannot remember the player's full name, though his last name was Johnson and he was a bonus baby. They gave him $125,000 to sign. That was a lot of money. They gave me $500. First pitch, the ball hits me and I go down on the ground. It was the worst pain I have ever felt in my life.

I was down on the ground for I don't know how long. My stomach was burning. They took me to the hospital and I spent three days laid up with a bag of ice on my testicle. Three days later the traveling secretary showed up with a plane ticket for me to go to Sanford, Florida, again. I checked out of the hospital, but I was in so much pain I don't know how I got to Sanford. The plane made so many stops I was lucky I figured out where I was supposed to go. I had to go through Miami and take a bus, but I got there.

Going back to Sanford was one of the worst things. I couldn't do anything there. I spent a month going to the doctor every day, but I could not pitch. They could have kept me in Phoenix another week or so, which would have been so much better. I was back in Sanford where there was nothing to do and there were racist attitudes.

It was much better after I was sent to Tacoma. I don't know how many Latin people they have there, but they seemed glad I was there. They liked me a lot. In fact, years later on the 25th anniversary of my playing with Tacoma, they invited me back to be part of the celebration. I had spent only a month or two of my life with Tacoma, but 25 years later they flew me to Seattle and had a helicopter waiting for me at the airport to take me to Tacoma.

There was a game going on and the stadium was packed. We landed right behind the pitcher's mound—during the game. We were late, but they stopped the game to have me go to the mound and throw a "first" pitch even though it wasn't a first pitch anymore. That was something I will never forget, the way the people were so happy to see me.

To be appreciated like that was something special, especially after my time in Sanford. It was so different. Those people in Tacoma cared about you as a human being. Not every place in the country was used to Latin players yet. I was not the first Latin player in the majors. I was not the first Latin player with the Giants. But there were still just a handful of Latin players in 1960.

After I recovered from the line drive, I pitched well in Tacoma. The Giants called me up to the major league roster on July 10, 1960.

CHAPTER 4

The Giant
from an Island Nation

*W*hen Juan Marichal received his long-awaited call-up to the majors—at least it seemed long-awaited to him—he was excited and felt prepared to pitch for the Giants. He was still adjusting to the English language, the United States, and the differences between his upbringing and the ways of his new country.

He still had strong allegiances to his home country, of course, and coming back to Laguna Verde after a summer of playing baseball in the United States was always a great moment for him. And with greater success in the States came greater celebrity in the Dominican. Marichal wasn't the first baseball player from the Dominican to make it in the major leagues—that honor went to Ozzie Virgil Sr., *who joined the Giants in 1956—but he quickly established himself as one of the best. And in a country with such tremendous passion for the sport, a successful player can reach heroic stature.*

The major league accomplishments of Marichal, his compadre Felipe Alou, and numerous other countrymen during the 1960s and 1970s sparked an incredible surge in Dominican baseball players in later decades, but Marichal never forgot the trials he had to endure to get to where he is today—the National Baseball Hall of Fame. Hard work, dedication, and a commitment to excellence, to being the best at what you do, are all important themes for Marichal that he tries to instill in younger generations.

Of equal importance to Marichal, something that is integral to his very nature, is a positive outlook. You will often find him with a smile on his face or using such words as beautiful *to describe something, because, as he explains, that is how he feels inside. "I am a happy person," he says, "and I like happy people." Considering some of the challenges he encountered in his life, first as a young boy growing up in circumstances that could be described as poverty despite the abundance of food on the family farm, and then as a young man in a strange country, his optimistic attitude is inspiring.*

Marichal's home country also went through some turbulent times in the early 1960s. The assassination of Rafael Trujillo in 1961 ended a long period of brutal and violent rule, but it also brought uncertainty and insta-bility to the island nation, something that Marichal was witnessing from afar. Although the 23-year-old had secured his place in the Giants' rotation, he arrived at spring training in Phoenix distracted by issues in his personal life. When he went back to the United States, he left behind his fiancée, Alma Caraval, in Santo Domingo. They kept in good communication via long-distance telephone calls, but it wasn't enough.

Marichal and Caraval had known each other for about two years, but she was only 17 and they didn't plan to marry until the following October. She could not come to the United States and spend the season with him. So after Marichal asked permission of new manager Alvin Dark, he took a few days off during spring training of 1962 and pushed up the wedding date.

Marichal flew from Phoenix to Houston to Miami to Santo Domingo. He spent three days in the Dominican and then retraced his steps with his bride.

Once the couple returned, Marichal settled into married life and soon made his true breakthrough as a star pitcher in the major leagues.

THE SEASON WAS HALF OVER WHEN I GOT CALLED UP TO JOIN THE GIANTS IN JULY 1960. BILL RIGNEY HAD BEEN FIRED, and the manager for the rest of the season was Tom Sheehan. He was just filling in. He told me right away I was just going to pitch batting practice for a week and that I would make my first start on July 19 against the Phillies. I had plenty of time to get ready.

After I threw a one-hitter in my first game—I will never forget that—the Giants started pitching me regularly and I ended up going 6–2. I was very proud of my first experience in the majors.

When I made it to the Giants, the people at home were very, very positive. That was still a very special thing to the people back home and all over the Dominican Republic. You know, to be on that list, such a small list of good Latin players who made it, even some who had been there before me and not made it to stay, it was special.

Every time a new Latin player got to the major leagues, the sportswriters wrote in the newspapers that he was going to be a superstar. I read it in every newspaper about me. They congratulated the person who signed me, Horacio Martinez, for his vision. At the end of the year, after the team sent me from Sanford to Tacoma to San Francisco, the Giants were invited to Japan and I got to pitch there, too, so they could see the "great" Juan Marichal, I think. That was a great, great experience.

People in the Dominican have strong allegiances to their local teams, but they love baseball and they follow the majors, too. If a team in the majors does well and Dominican players are stars on the team, it gets even more support back home.

There was already a connection with the Giants when I got there because of Felipe Alou, and there has been strong support for the Giants as long as I have been around. When I played with the

Giants, every game I pitched in the majors was broadcast back to the Dominican. A few years ago when the Red Sox won the World Series, two of their biggest stars were David "Big Papi" Ortiz and Manny Ramirez. They are from the Dominican, and fans adopted their team.

I had teased my mother that one day she would hear my name on the radio, and I was right. She was happy about that. Right from the beginning, when I was in the minor leagues, I sent money home to her. In the minors I made $300 a month. From that $300 I sent her $50 every 15 days. I sent her $100 a month. I was happy that I could help her by being a baseball player. Even that little bit of money helped her, and that was before I made a major league salary. I think she started to like baseball. When I returned home and pitched in the Dominican, my mother would come to the games.

My older brothers and I tried to talk her into coming to some of my games in San Francisco, but she wouldn't do it. I tried so many times. She used to say to me, "Son, don't bother. You know I don't want to be on those airplanes. No way are you gonna get me in those planes." She never flew.

One thing about the Dominican people, and it is the same for the ballplayers, is we love our country very much. If the Dominican people go outside of the country, they show their pride in being Dominican, and they can't wait to get back. Even the players of today, they make so much money playing the game, but as soon as the season ends, they come home. They may be finished playing at eight o'clock, and at midnight they are catching a plane back to the Dominican. They love home.

People in the Latin American countries that follow sports are very proud of their country's athletes. Not only baseball players. It can be a boxer. It can be a tennis player. It can be any sport. They speak very highly about them. I think the baseball players are on top, though. You know, it can be a great architect, too, and we have a great many doctors. The people are just proud of Dominicans when they accomplish something, because we love our own people. There is always a strong feeling of "He is one of ours." The people have very high respect for a baseball player who makes it to the major leagues.

In my day, when I was young and started to play baseball, families did not like to see their daughters get involved with baseball players. Now it is different. The president of the country might throw a party at his house for baseball players. Every time a group of athletes goes to different countries to represent our country, they go to compete with a flag that the president has given them as he wishes them all the luck in the world. He asks them to behave and represent the country well and win for their country. It is as if the president has given them a blessing.

We are a colorful people. The women wear bright dresses, blue, pink, yellow. There are many colorful buildings in Santo Domingo. I think that is part of the national character, the idea of bright colors. The people like to show life, a happy life, and they show off with their favorite color. If you go around the Dominican, especially in the resort areas, you will see many men wearing colorful shirts, too.

It is very fresh. Beautiful. That is how I feel about life, too. I like happy people. I believe whatever is happening in my life, in a positive way, is because of God. When I talk to youngsters sometimes they look at me like I am a god because I played in the major leagues. They forget how I got there, all the work that we all have to do to get there. I don't want anybody to think it is impossible. It is possible for them, too, if they work hard. I don't want them to forget that.

That is the word I stress to the kids: *Possible*. I tell them that when I grew up we had no money, how I played my first organized game, how I got into the Air Force, how I went to Springfield, Tacoma, the Giants, and into the Hall of Fame. I tell them, "If I could travel this route to get there, then nothing is impossible—nothing—because if I did it, all of you can do it." It depends on what is in you, what you want to be. Whatever you want to be, you can do it if you try. I decided to go for baseball. I think I got to the top.

When I was going up in baseball, and even when I got to the majors, I didn't want to be just one of the group. I wanted to be one of the best. Once I got to the majors I learned who was the best hitter, who was the best pitcher, and who was the best infielder. I learned all of that when I got there, and I felt I wanted to be one of them.

In my first year with the Giants, I learned what the competition was first-hand and I succeeded, and I kept on learning. You get more confident each time you succeed. After a while you look around and see who else is pitching and you think, "I want to be the best. I want to be better than everyone. I want to win more."

When I got to the major leagues I learned about Sandy Koufax, Warren Spahn, and Don Drysdale, all the big names. I said to myself, "They started where I did and look where they are. So if I work hard, I think I've got a chance to be at that level." That is the top of the top. They are all in the Hall of Fame.

But let me tell you, it's not easy. You have to work hard and you have to sacrifice. Some players are good, but they are not the best because they do not have discipline or are not willing to work harder. Look at Mickey Mantle, for example. I felt so sad when I heard what he said before he passed away, that he wished he had lived a different life. He said to young people, "Don't be like me." That was so sad.

He was talking about drinking. That really hurt me when I heard that man say that he could have been better if he lived a different life. A lot of pitchers love to drink and love to party. But if you want to be the best, you can't do it.

You have to make choices about how to live every day. Young players whose families do not have much money come from the Dominican to the United States, and suddenly they have so much money. They go from having nothing to becoming rich and famous. It's very, very tough to adjust. The important thing to the people is that no matter how much money you make, how famous you are, you do not change your behavior. It is important to be the same guy you were when you were growing up. That's what people look to see.

When I signed with the Giants I got $500. Now kids who sign at 16 years old get $4.5 million. I try to talk to young players who sign these big contracts if I disagree with what I see they are doing with their lives. They don't know how to handle the money and the fame. Many of them need somebody to talk to.

Sometimes these young players become arrogant. They have a lot of money and they become full of themselves. There was a kid who got about $3 million from the Giants. He was playing on a team in the Dominican, and after a game they went to a bar to have a beer. He is in this bar and he gets into a fight over a chair with another guy about the same age. There was an argument, and this player pulled out a gun and killed the other guy. Killed him! Now he's out of baseball.

That kind of thing has happened three or four times already. The young players get that kind of money, and some people are smart and they live on it and become superstars, but others don't know how to handle it and it's sad. That really hurts me.

The Dominican is not a rich country, and if a player has the opportunity to make his family rich then it is good that he gets the money. But if he gets so much money and cannot handle it, it's just a waste. It's a big loss for him, but also his family. It is a missed opportunity.

Now, there are so many Dominicans in the majors. In 50 years, there has been huge change. Now one of the main things the Dominican Republic is known for is producing baseball players. Now when you mention the Dominican Republic, one of the first things people think of is baseball.

We have had many baseball players who have made millions of dollars. When Sammy Sosa was hitting all those home runs for the Chicago Cubs, he started a foundation to help people in the Dominican, and he donated help when there was a hurricane. The country named a highway right in front of the airport for Sammy. It's Route 66 and the most home runs he hit in one year was 66, so it was renamed "Sammy Sosa Highway."

Pedro Martinez, who is a friend of mine and was such a great pitcher for the Montreal Expos and Boston Red Sox, is from Santo Domingo. He bought a piece of land there and built a school and an outpatient medical center, or clinic, for the people. His foundation raises money and makes it easier for people to get wheelchairs and other medical equipment through the clinic.

For more than 25 years I have organized an annual golf tournament to raise money for different charities. Each year we give money to two different causes. This past year one cause was *Un Techo para Mi Pais*, a foundation that builds homes for the impoverished, and the other was *Aldea del Niño*, an organization for underprivileged kids in the town of San Francisco de Macoris.

About 15 or 20 years ago the city named a street after me. It's a small street called "Juan Marichal Street." It is near the Botanical Garden in Santo Domingo. One of my grandchildren, Marco, who is seven years old, passes that street every day on his way to school. He sees the name and says, "Oh, that's Papapa's street."

I have been so lucky to be able to do things to help people in the Dominican after becoming a professional ballplayer.

When I came home in the offseason I was very excited. I missed the Dominican. I knew that I was going to see my family and sleep in my own bed. I feel the same way now. I am going to see my grandchildren and sleep in my own bed. I get so relaxed when I am sleeping in my bed.

When you travel and sleep in different hotels, it's not the same. That's why coming home is the best. I love San Francisco and I love my country. I love going to the place where I was born at the farm. Now when I go, I feel 10 or 15 years younger.

I get to see old friends and I see the river. That is like an old friend. There are always good memories, too. My wife, Alma, was a neighbor of the Alou family, and she was good friends with the sisters.

At the time I was playing for the Dominican Air Force, I used to go to the Alous' neighborhood to see them and our other friend Chichi Garcia. When I first saw Alma I thought how beautiful she was, but she was only 15 years old. I liked her right from the beginning, but we would just say hi and had nothing but a friendship.

Oh, she looked so great. People didn't believe her age. I saw her almost every day when I went from the Air Force base to the city and we got to be good friends. I got to be good friends with her whole family. I called her father Papa Jose and her mother Doña Polonia. Her father and I were like father and son. That was great and her mother was nice, too. I got to meet all her sisters. There are five sisters and one boy.

A man named Jose Garcia Trujillo, one of the Trujillo family, used to visit the house, too, and he was like an uncle to Alma. Alma and I were getting to be a little bit more romantic, a little bit more than friends. This Trujillo man loved baseball. Every time he came to Alma's house he sent somebody to get me and bring me there to talk baseball. We spent a lot of time talking baseball. He used to drink vodka. I did not drink and I did not want to drink, but he always offered me drinks and I was afraid to say no to him. He was a general. That was tough. Gradually, he accepted me. We got close because of talking baseball.

Alma and I had a secret then. We decided we were engaged, but we didn't tell anyone.

One day I was coming to her house to visit, and when I got to the neighborhood all of Alma's sisters and friends were in front of the house on a little wall that we used to climb. The general came along. We saw his car stop and he went into the house. About 10 minutes later he sent for me to come in. We're all there and the general told Papa Jose and Doña Polonia that Alma and I were kissing in the street. Oh my God, I was so embarrassed when he said that. I didn't know where to hide my face.

Everything was old-fashioned then. Papa Jose and Doña Polonia looked at me and said, "I told my daughters that any time they fall in love with somebody to bring him to the house." I had been to the house and they knew me, but they didn't know Alma and I were engaged. When the general told them that we were kissing, that gave me the freedom to let them know that Alma and I liked each other. So after that, the engagement was known.

We kept dating when I was in the Dominican, but Alma was still very young. Before I left for the United States for spring training in 1962, my brother, who came with me to the house sometimes, said, "Let's marry these two before Juan goes to spring training." I said, "No, no, I have to concentrate on baseball right now. I don't want to get married yet."

At that time the Dominican was going through a bad political crisis. Rafael Trujillo, the country's leader, had been killed and nobody knew what was going to happen next. There was a lot of political unrest. People knew that Papa Jose and Doña Polonia were related to the Trujillos.

I had flown to spring training, but I was seeing all these things on the TV news and reading about what was going on, and I was getting worried about Alma and her family. People who had been angry about Trujillo were calling Papa Jose and Doña Polonia names and saying they should get out of their house. I was homesick and upset. I was very worried about what was going to happen.

So I went to Alvin Dark, the manager—this was in March of 1962—and asked him if I could go home and get married because then I could bring Alma from the Dominican to the United States. It was such a bad situation, but she couldn't just leave and join me without being married. She was still 17. Dark asked if she could leave the Dominican and come to Phoenix and if we could get married there. I said she couldn't because she was a minor.

He gave me permission. I flew to the Dominican at the beginning of a week, I stayed there for about three days, and then we flew back to Arizona. It was all very rushed, but we had a nice wedding and when we got back to Arizona it was wonderful. It was one of the best decisions I ever made.

But at the same time it was very hard for Alma. She was worried about the rest of her family and what would happen. It was her first time away from the Dominican Republic. It was a very, very delicate situation. I had to reassure her that her family was going to be all right, but she cried many, many times.

She didn't speak English, either. Alma was in a new country, young, married, and she did not speak the language. It was a very tough situation for her. I was lucky that I had some friends in the area from Nicaragua and El Salvador and she could speak Spanish with them. And then, when we came out of spring training and moved to San Francisco, I sent for her mother. She spent time with us. One time I sent for one of her sisters. In those days in baseball we had much longer road trips. One of them was 24 days on the road. Now the longest is about six days.

When Alma's family was there she was okay because she wasn't living by herself when I traveled with the Giants. At times when I was on road trips and no members of her family were visiting, she would stay at friends' houses. She was afraid to stay in our house alone. At times it was a very rough situation.

These days the Dominican is a growing country with many beach resorts, and tourists come from all over. When I was young things were a lot different, although when I was growing up I didn't really understand how the country worked. Rafael Trujillo was a dictator and he ran everything. I didn't know anything about it. I was a kid living on a farm outside the city where I could take care of cows or goats and go swimming and play baseball. That's what I knew.

When I was summoned to be in the Air Force I still didn't really know about Trujillo except that he ran everything and if he wanted something done, you had to do it. When that lieutenant came to our house to tell me to join the Air Force, we knew it was "an order from God." My mother is the one who really knew. But I was 18 years old and I didn't know that he was bad. I just knew that Trujillo was a really powerful man.

We thought our president was a hero, that he was a general who had been brave and famous and that's how he became president.

After I left the country for Sanford, Florida, and spring training, I began to learn more about Trujillo. Other Latin Americans there mocked him. I guess when he was young he used to save bottle caps like from Coca-Cola or Pepsi and put them on his clothes like medals. Then when he was an adult he put real medals on his clothes. Other Latins teased us about Trujillo and made fun of us, as if we wanted to put bottle caps on our clothes like heroes.

These same players from other Latin countries started telling us about Trujillo, that Trujillo was bad, that Trujillo was a killer, and that Trujillo assassinated a lot of people. This was all completely new to me. We never talked about such things in the Dominican.

It was much later when I heard the story about the Negro League players coming to the Dominican to play for Trujillo and spending a night in jail before the championship game; they feared they might get shot if they didn't win the championship for Trujillo. I didn't doubt it. When you got to know the whole story about Trujillo and the people who surrounded him, it was clear that they were trouble. So many things happened that I didn't learn until afterwards.

Early in my career with the Giants, I was still getting used to living in the United States. Just like when I was in the minors, I went to live with a family in San Francisco. Matty Alou and I lived with a woman named Blanche Johnson and her husband; they didn't have kids.

We had a good friendship with the Johnsons. We loved those people and they loved us. Mrs. Johnson was a great lady. She told me that I had two mothers. She said, "You have a mother in the Dominican and you have a mother here." It was like she adopted us. When I got there she took some towels and stitched the words "My Baby" on them, and those were my towels. Nobody else could use those towels. Mrs. Johnson worked at American Can Company, but before she went to work she cooked for us. She was more than a mother. That lady was very special. She helped us learn English.

My English was still not very good when I came to San Francisco. When I left the Dominican the first time, I knew nothing. I could say "hello" and I knew a few phrases that I could use in a restaurant. At first, in Michigan City or Springfield, I would go into a restaurant with my teammates and I could not order my food. One of them would order something and I would say, "Same." I just repeated that.

I remember hearing about one Latin player on a team in the United States who didn't know any English and he ate at Denny's because they had pictures of all the food, and he just pointed to what he wanted. That was pretty good.

Mrs. Johnson used to make me speak English, and she used to bring me books to use, a dictionary of English/Spanish and Spanish/English, and that's how I learned. I also spoke a lot with my American teammates. I knew if I talked to them I would learn more phrases. If I only talked to Matty or Felipe Alou, we would talk Spanish. Some players were very nice. They said, "Don't be afraid to say anything back to us because we can correct you and we can teach you how to pronounce it."

Two guys who helped me a lot were Jack Sanford, the pitcher, and Jim Davenport, our third baseman. He's from the South, from Alabama, but he was very friendly. I have so much respect for him.

One day we were playing in Houston—they were the Colt .45s still—and some guys in the stands were drunk. I knew they were drunk, and when I was going to the bench from the mound or when Felipe was coming in from the outfield, they would yell things at us. One thing they yelled was, "Hey, you, Kennedy's boy!" John F. Kennedy was president and they were yelling this at us because of his support for civil rights. Sanford and Davenport went up into the stands and had a fight with the guys. They did this for us, on our behalf. I will never forget that. I had a real good relationship with Jim Davenport, and many of the other Giants were like that, too.

I knew I had to improve my English. I felt bad any time somebody wanted to talk with me and I needed an interpreter. I kept telling myself, "You have to learn, you have to learn, you have to learn." I could understand what people wanted to tell me, but I didn't speak English very well. I got by, but I had lots of practice. Mrs. Johnson made sure of that.

CHAPTER 5

Glory Days

*J*uan Marichal signed with an organization that was rich not only in Latin American talent but in talent in general. The first meant he was welcomed to the majors by a group of players who literally spoke his language and could help him comfortably make the transition from a naive to knowledgeable young man. The second meant that the Giants could win a pennant and reach the World Series, as they did in 1962, and continue to challenge for top honors throughout the 1960s.

At one point in the early 1960s, the Giants had five future Hall of Famers on the team at the same time. Besides Marichal, there was Willie Mays, whom some consider the greatest player of all time; slugger Willie McCovey, producer of 521 career home runs; 300-game winner Gaylord Perry; and Orlando Cepeda.

In an era before National and American League championship series and divisional play with wildcard teams, only one team in each league was rewarded with a postseason berth, and that postseason berth was the World Series. Being the best in the regular season counted for more back then. It also meant that the window of opportunity was a very narrow one. You could win 100 games and lose the pennant by one game, and without tiers of playoffs you were the odd one out. You had a great season and all it meant was that you would watch the World Series on television, just like the players on the eighth-place team did.

At the same time that the Giants were anchored by such top-caliber players, the Los Angeles Dodgers were equally loaded. It was like the old New York City rivalry all over again, just transplanted to the West Coast. Dodgers versus Giants, as if it were a subway series instead of a short-jet-hop series. The Dodgers featured ace pitchers Sandy Koufax and Don Drysdale, also on their way to the Hall of Fame, and slugging outfielder Duke Snider. Maury Wills set base-stealing records.

Some of the greatest ballplayers whom Marichal ever saw were either in the clubhouse with him or frequent foes from down the California coast.

Marichal was fast establishing his own place within that circle of greats. During his first half-season with the Giants in 1960, he finished 6–2 and posted a 2.66 earned run average in 81⅓ innings. He surrendered just 59 hits and 24 earned runs while issuing just 28 walks compared to 58 strikeouts. These numbers represented early signs of mastery.

In 1961, Marichal was a member of the big club from the start. No more minor league spring training adventures. He was being counted on as a member of the starting rotation of the San Francisco Giants. He won 13 games while striking out 124 batters and walking 48 in 185 innings. His 3.89 ERA was better than that of veteran starters Jack Sanford and Billy Loes.

The improvement continued during the pennant season of 1962. He started 36 games, completed 18 of them, and finished with a record of 18–11. His ratio of strikeouts to walks was third best in the National League. Although he had to leave the game in the fourth inning due to injury, the 24-year-old Marichal got to enjoy the ultimate thrill of starting a game on baseball's greatest stage, in the World Series.

I FINISHED MY ROOKIE YEAR IN THE MAJOR LEAGUES IN 1960, AND I WAS READY FOR A FULL YEAR WITH THE GIANTS, BUT 1961 turned out to be a so-so year. I was still learning and I needed to get better.

The next year was a great one for the Giants and for me, starting with my getting married during spring training. That year I made real progress toward becoming a good pitcher. I won 18 games in 1962 and we went to the World Series.

The Giants had only been in San Francisco for a few years, so the team still felt new to the area. The Giants had a long history, but for the people in San Francisco, I don't think they cared about what happened in New York. They didn't want to hear about that. There were only a few connections to New York. Carl Hubbell was a very well-respected man in the organization, and Willie Mays came from New York. Wes Westrum had been a player in New York and now he was a coach in San Francisco. Hubbell didn't say much. He was a quiet man. But we all knew Willie was a hero in New York.

Carl Hubbell was one of the scouts from the organization who went around to each team and watched the players. Then he wrote reports. He talked to the players and coaches and managers, but he hardly talked.

Sometimes I wondered why he didn't talk to me more and why other coaches didn't talk to me more. I felt badly at the time, because I wondered if it was a racial problem. I found out later it wasn't. I was talking to some other guys about how I was worried about this and one of them said, "You know why they never come and talk to you? Because Carl told every instructor to never come close to you and tell you anything. Because your talent is natural." That's what I found out that day, and I was very relieved. He just didn't want people to mess with my style.

Later I heard that from the first moment Hubbell saw me in Sanford, Florida, he told people, "That kid has natural talent." He didn't want anyone to bother with my form.

The 1962 team was a great team. We had Willie Mays, Willie McCovey, and Orlando Cepeda. Wow, they could hit. They're all in the Hall of Fame. We had Ed Bailey and Tom Haller as catchers. Jim Ray Hart—he was a great hitter, too—and Jim Davenport. Jose Pagan was the shortstop. Chuck Hiller played second base. My old friend Felipe Alou played right field.

Our biggest problem was how to play Orlando and Willie McCovey at the same time. They were really both first basemen, so to play them at once one had to play the outfield and neither one of them liked that. We needed a designated hitter rule, but there wasn't one. That would have been something.

Our other pitchers were Jack Sanford, Bob Bolin, and Billy Pierce, and Stu Miller was in the bullpen. He was a little guy. He weighed 165 pounds and there is a famous story about the wind blowing him off the mound in the All-Star Game in 1961. He was called for a balk. Of course, that game was at Candlestick Park. That was the Giants' home park and it was always windy there, especially in the late afternoon. What did somebody say? The worst winter I ever spent was a summer in San Francisco.

You know, one day we were taking batting practice in the big, heavy batting cage and I saw the wind move it from one side to the other. We used to play a game when we were in the outfield. We took a glove and put it on the right-field wall, and the wind was so strong it would keep it there. The wind would just hold it in place. That was something.

But Candlestick Park was my home field. I figured if hitters hated the place, then I should like it. I was going to be prepared for the wind and not think about whether the day was windy or not, or whether it was 30 degrees or not. My problem is when I face the batter. I knew that the batters wanted to warm up their hands. I just wanted to throw the pitch. I liked it when a pitch hurt the batter's hands at the start of the game. I tried to get their hands to sting right from the beginning. Then they wouldn't want to go back and hit.

The wind was supposed to be bad for pitchers, but I knew I had to make it work for me instead of against me. The wind was real, but every time I went out to the mound I had to think positive all the time. If you think negative, only negative things are going to come out.

Some hitters used to joke around and say about me, "This guy was so mean at Candlestick Park that when he sees somebody at the plate, he keeps shaking off the sign because he wants to get dust in our eyes before he throws the ball." All of this puts doubt in their minds, and it's hard for them to hit if they think that way.

We were fighting the Dodgers from the start in our pennant-winning 1962 season. It was not exactly the same, but with the Giants moving from New York to San Francisco and the Dodgers moving from Brooklyn to Los Angeles there was still a rivalry. It was the first year the Dodgers played at Dodger Stadium in Chavez Ravine. Now it's one of the oldest ballparks in the majors.

We went back and forth with the Dodgers that season. We were in first place and one game ahead, and then we were one game behind. In the end we tied and had to have a best-of-three playoff to decide the pennant.

We won the first game in San Francisco and the Dodgers won the next. I was pitching the third game at Chavez Ravine. We were behind 4–2 when I left after the seventh inning, but we scored four runs in the ninth to win the pennant to reach the World Series. We flew back to San Francisco that night. Everyone was going crazy, they were so happy. They parked our plane back from the gate and brought out five buses to get out of the airport because of the size of the crowd. This was San Francisco's first pennant, so they wanted to have a big party.

After beating the Dodgers we went straight to the World Series to play the New York Yankees. We knew how good they were, but we tried not to be afraid of them. The year before, Roger Maris had broken Babe Ruth's season home run record with 61. They were terrific with Mickey Mantle, Tony Kubek, Tom Tresh, Clete Boyer, Bobby Richardson, and Bill Skowron. Great team.

My turn to pitch against the Yankees came in the fourth game of the 1962 World Series. Two things happened in that game, one of them funny and one of them so sad that I am going to carry it in my mind forever.

We were playing in Yankee Stadium and I was winning 2–0 and the Giants were hitting in the fifth inning. We had men on first and third with no outs. I came to the plate and the dugout gave me the bunt sign. Ball one, and the bunt sign was still on.

Whitey Ford, the Yankees' great pitcher, was on the mound. Ball two. Fake bunt sign, ball three. Fake bunt sign, strike one. Fake bunt sign, strike two. Then I got a sign I thought I would never get. They gave me the squeeze play sign on a 3-2 count. Tom Haller was on third and Jose Pagan on first. I was trying to bunt Haller home.

One more ball and I could walk and we would have the bases loaded. The ball headed straight for my ankle, but because the squeeze play was on and the runners were going with the pitch, I had to try to make contact. To me, it was a stupid play because you don't want a double play with me bunting all the way. But the squeeze?

The ball was nowhere near the strike zone. It tailed in and hit my finger on the bat. I had to leave the game right away, and that was it. I had been pitching the best game of my life. I had struck out Mickey Mantle twice.

It was raining hard for four days in the middle of the Series in San Francisco. The whole World Series took 13 days to play because of the weather, and because it went seven games. We had rain in both cities. One team went out to Modesto to work out and the other went to Fresno. Candlestick Park was like a pool of water, it rained so much. To try and dry the field they brought in three helicopters, which hovered really low over the grass. That's how they thought they could dry it out so we could play. Only they wrecked the infield dirt. So they decided to pour gasoline over the dirt and set it on fire. That's how they dried out the field and we played the final game.

The field was not completely dry anyway. Willie Mays hit a ball to right field and when it landed on the grass, it stuck. If the field had not been wet, the ball would have gone all the way to the wall. Willie could have made it to third base and we could have tied the game. We lost 1–0.

Just getting to the World Series as such a young pitcher was very special. We won the game that I had to leave, but without that injury I could have been the winning pitcher.

In the ninth inning of the seventh game it felt like we could win. Everybody remembers what happened. Willie McCovey hit the ball so hard it seemed like a rocket. Bobby Richardson was playing second base and he lunged to the left and caught the ball. I was in the dugout watching. I thought the ball was going too fast to catch. If Willie hit that ball a little higher it would have landed in the ocean. He hit it that hard. But the Yankees were supposed to win, so he didn't. Things happen because that's the way they are supposed to be. People say, "Oh, if it was only a few inches higher." But that's the game of baseball.

Everybody in our dugout jumped up for the hit, but you could see the disappointment on people's faces after it was caught. It was very sudden. It was very quick. The ball was hit so hard it almost knocked Bobby Richardson over. You remember those words, "The thrill of victory and the agony of defeat," from *Wide World of Sports*? That was what it was like.

Willie hit the ball so hard that he never even took one step toward first base. Before he moved, Richardson had already caught the ball. Willie did not say anything, but Willie is a very quiet man. The Yankees had been so good for so long and had won so much, everyone thought they would win every year. They were the best team in baseball. It would have been nice to beat them.

We had such a great team. I thought we would get back to the World Series many times, but we never did. You look at the list of the Hall of Famers on that team and you might think, these guys can't lose. Five Hall of Famers on the same team. After 1962, I thought, "I'm going to be back here. Next time we will win the World Series. We'll be there. We'll be there." But there was always another team that played better than us, and that's why they won.

I had an okay relationship with Alvin Dark, who became the Giants' manager before the 1961 season and stayed through 1964. He was good to me when he let me go home to get married in 1962, but sometimes I didn't understand him. To some players, he was mean. When you do something for me, I feel good about it. I never forgot that he gave me permission to leave spring training to get married. He did good things.

One year I arrived at spring training underweight by about 10 pounds. He used to tell me to eat to get my weight back up to the 180s. He would sit with me while I drank Coca-Cola or a vanilla milkshake. He said, "Hey kid, you've got to eat this." That is the good side of Alvin Dark. He also had a hard side.

He was from the South and he quoted the Bible a lot. But he said one thing that was so incredibly stupid in an interview that we couldn't believe it. It started with a play on which Orlando made a mistake, and in the dugout after the game Alvin tried explain to a sportswriter from *Newsday* why things weren't working for us.

Dark said, "We have trouble because we have so many Negro and Spanish-speaking ballplayers on this team. They are just not able to perform up to the white ballplayers when it comes to mental alertness. You can't make most Negro and Spanish players have the pride in their team that you can get from white players."

I felt sorry for him. It was just weird. I didn't let it bother me, because what he did for me was still the most important thing in my memories. It was a very stupid thing, but those things happen. A similar incident happened with Al Campanis from the Dodgers years later. For years this guy had showed the world how he loved black ballplayers. Then he says one wrong thing and gets fired. He made a mistake. I don't understand how this happens.

In the clubhouse, I thought of Alvin Dark as a happy guy, but one who hated to lose. He was famous for being hard-nosed as a ballplayer. One time we came into the clubhouse after a loss and we had a dinner spread out for us on the table. He came over and pulled the tablecloth with one hand and, whoosh, threw everything on the floor.

For those of us who grew up in the Dominican or other places where we did not have a lot of money, it was a sin to waste food. Felipe Alou was walking up behind Alvin and he immediately bent down to the floor, picked up some food and began eating it. He just looked at Alvin and said, "You're not supposed to throw food away." He did that with a lot of dignity and it was a very serious statement. There are people all over the world who are hungry. "When people are starving, you don't throw food away."

Felipe was saying, essentially, "If you are mad at us, then throw a chair instead. Break a chair." Once in Philadelphia, we were coming into the clubhouse after a game and Alvin grabbed one of those wooden stools, a footstool. They have metal around the edge. He grabbed it, picked it up, and threw it at the wall, and it came up as he was throwing it and it caught his finger. He tore off part of his little finger. It just came off. We had to find it and pick it up and take it to the doctor and they sewed it back on.

He was a competitor. He didn't like to lose. Nobody likes to lose, but he was getting too angry.

He did one more dumb thing. He said nobody could speak Spanish in the clubhouse. We didn't understand what he was trying to do. If I am going to talk to Felipe Alou, whom I have known most of my life from the Dominican, we are going to speak Spanish. If I am going to talk to Orlando from Puerto Rico, of course we are going to speak Spanish.

I don't believe he thought forbidding us to speak Spanish would make us better or help us win. I think he just felt we had too many Latins on the team and he felt left out when we were talking.

He didn't know what we were talking about and thought maybe we were talking about him. I just think he believed we had too many Latin players.

One time we were playing in St. Louis against the Cardinals. At that time we had seven Latin players. The Latin players did not go out and party at night. Some of us were not drinkers at all. There was a curfew on the road and something came out in a San Francisco paper saying seven players were out late and had broken curfew. The story said that it was the Latin players. In fact, none was a Latin player, but everybody got the idea it was the Latin players because it was seven guys.

We felt bad because there was no use for that. That's something you write when you want to hurt somebody, when you want to do something bad to someone. Did Alvin Dark say something to the writer? I don't know. Somebody had to tell the sportswriter something. My wife knew right away I wasn't one of the guys out partying, breaking curfew, because I didn't drink. But that creates doubts in people's minds.

Another time we were playing the Braves in Milwaukee and the night before the game our manager gave Orlando $500 to take us out to dinner. So we went out and had a good dinner and felt good about it. I don't know why Dark chose us. Maybe we were doing a good job. Maybe he just wanted us to have a good time. Well, the next day Orlando wasn't playing. I think it was in the ninth inning he put Orlando in to pinch-hit for somebody. Orlando hit the ball to the shortstop, but he couldn't run so he was late to first base and he was out. Dark fined him $500. That meant Orlando had paid for our dinner. Orlando was furious. He was so mad. Orlando did not like Alvin Dark very much.

I didn't have that much trouble with Alvin. I know what he said. People make mistakes. I'm the type of person who believes that if you make a mistake, you should pay for it, but not forever.

Alma and I loved San Francisco. The people, the city. Everyone treated us wonderfully. They cheered me at the ballpark, and when we went out to the movies people recognized me. Alma and I went to restaurants all over the place. We used to get invited to Reno, to Lake Tahoe, everything. I never gambled, so we used to go there for fun to see the shows and the big stars. I met Elvis and Priscilla Presley in Las Vegas once. I think that was the biggest day of my life. I am a very big fan of Elvis, and so is my daughter Elsie. I saw him at least five times.

When Alma and I came home after meeting him for the first time, my daughters were so excited. They kept asking me, "What is he like? What does he look like?" I told them, "He is the handsomest man in the world." Elsie went wild. She loved him so much.

The first four children Alma and I had together were girls: Alma Rose, Elsie, Yvette, and Ursula Raquel, who was named after actresses Ursula Andress and Raquel Welch. I was always outnumbered in the house. Then we had two more children after I retired, Charlene and Juan Antonio.

I used to sign autographs everywhere in San Francisco. Even now, years after I finished playing, whenever I go to San Francisco people ask me for autographs. I never said no to autographs because I know what it means. When I was a kid, my brother took me to see my first professional soccer game in the Dominican. When I saw those players, they seemed like something out of this world. To me, they looked like gods, and being close to them was enough to get me excited. So I know how people look at players and feel about players. They feel the same way about baseball players now.

I feel badly when I see some player or ex-player asked for an autograph and he says no. I think when a kid comes up to you and asks you for an autograph, you should sign something. Let the kid be happy.

Being a young man in San Francisco in the 1960s, it was a very interesting time for me. I had only come from the Dominican Republic a few years earlier. I didn't know many things, and I was a young, married man as well as trying to make it in baseball. But I was doing well and that got me attention in San Francisco. People started to recognize me and I felt great. It was exciting.

Everywhere Willie Mays went, there was a mob. I was playing with so many greats—Felipe, Orlando, Willie McCovey—and it made me feel like one of them, that I was on the same level as they were, when people started to welcome me.

One time on a road trip, I think it was in Philadelphia, a group of us went to the movies, and Orlando Cepeda fell asleep in the theater during the movie. When it ended we all got up and left Orlando there. You know at the end when they clean up and the ushers come through the theater. One of them shined the flashlight in his face and woke him up. Orlando was so mad at us. We were all waiting outside the theater for him, though. We had to explain to him what happened at the end of the movie.

After the Giants traded Orlando in 1966, we had two guys who always kept us laughing, pitchers Ray Sadecki and Mike McCormick. They would give other players "hot-foots" in the dugout, setting their shoes on fire. Somebody would get a guy real interested in what was going on out on the field, and then very slowly and smoothly they put the match in his shoes. When that flame reached your foot you started jumping. When those guys weren't playing, you had to watch out for them in the dugout.

There was another group in the bullpen that used to spit tobacco juice on the uniform of coach Andy Gilbert, but I didn't like that. I didn't think it was funny. I had a lot of respect for that man.

I see these baseball movies like *Bull Durham*, and they have these funny conversations on the mound, but that wasn't me. When I was on the mound, I thought about nothing except the game and the opposing players. I didn't want to mess around on the mound. I just wanted to concentrate on what I was doing.

Sometimes before a game we raced frogs. Someone would bring about 10 frogs to the park and we raced them. We bet on whose frog would win. Sometimes Willie Mays would bet. He never started these things, but he enjoyed it when we did them. Everyone had so much respect for Willie.

I was having fun in those days, and I was pitching good ball, and I think people liked me because I liked them. I always tried to be friendly to the fans, so I think we had something going back and forth. Right from the beginning the sportswriters treated me really well, too. They wrote a lot of articles about me and my family and the way I pitched. I think it all made it easy for me to be accepted there.

I loved to work out. I ran all during the offseason. It was easy to run outdoors in the Dominican in the winter. I used to visit Felipe,

Matty, and Jesus Alou and run on the beach where they lived. I ran five days a week. I would do my workout and then I would go fishing with Felipe and Jesus. I love to fish. When I lived in San Francisco I would carry a light pole around town with me.

I used to love to hunt, too. In San Francisco, this guy I knew who owned a restaurant used to take me out tracker hunting with dogs. Those dogs are amazing the way they hunt, how they stalk and bring back the birds, and the way they move themselves when they point and stand over a bird. If the bird is stopped, they stop. Sometimes you have to go up to the birds and scare them into flying while the dog stands there.

We hunted pheasants at a private club and the limit was eight. Then we brought them back to the restaurant and cleaned them and he put them in a bag for me. I would tell him he had to take some, but he would insist I take all 16. He said, "Don't worry, I got some in my freezer. Take them." My wife used to cook them. Oh my God, what a delicious bird.

In the Dominican I used to fish for apun. It's a big fish with a funny face. We have red snapper, too, that live near the beach. There are other fish we catch with a net, not a hook. You can fish for marlin. I caught a 125-pound marlin once. I have a friend who caught the biggest one in a particular year, about 600 pounds. It was in a tournament and he got a brand new Mercedes as a prize. Tarpon are an exciting fish. The tarpon can spit the hook right out of its mouth when jumping.

Over our friendship of many years, I have done many things with Felipe Alou. We used to scuba dive with a snorkel and mask where he lived when I did my offseason workouts. There is beautiful water, the Caribbean, there. On days that I didn't work out we used to leave the house at 4 A.M., get a boat, and go out on a bay scuba diving. We had spear guns with us to shoot fish.

One day we jumped off the boat and were swimming around, and all of a sudden I couldn't move. I had a bad cramp in my leg. We were in about 60 feet of water. It's an area like a canyon. You can't see the bottom. I was tremendously uncomfortable. No matter how shallow the water, you can't move. You can't do anything.

I did get to the surface and lucky for me Felipe was not too far from me. He was still pretty close to the boat looking for something to shoot. I got on top of the water and I hollered. It was a good thing he was nearby because I might have drowned. I was about 40 feet from the boat and he dragged me over. He grabbed me tight and had to work to get me to the boat. Felipe is a good swimmer, a really strong swimmer. It was definitely a scary moment for me.

I still have fishing equipment and hunting equipment, but I don't do those things as much as I used to do. I don't strike people out like I did in 1962, either.

CHAPTER 6

Mastering the Mound

*O*ne thing that Marichal faced as soon as he broke in with the Giants in 1960 were opponents' challenges to the legality of his pitching delivery. The high-kicking style was so unusual that batters didn't know what to make of it, and opposing managers didn't like it. By the time Marichal had raised his record to 3–0 in 1963 following an incredible, 16-inning pitcher's duel with Warren Spahn, the Milwaukee Braves were protesting whether his form was within the rules.

It wasn't the high-kick part they questioned. Braves manager Charlie Dressen, like so many team bosses always on alert for an edge, chose to attack where Marichal placed his foot on the pitching rubber. Dressen sought to get the umpires to force Marichal to place his foot on the middle of the rubber instead of on the corner so that his left foot was behind the rubber. It was all so much bunk to chief umpire Jocko Conlan, who rejected Dressen's third-inning plea, saying as long as Marichal had one foot on the rubber Conlan didn't care where he put the other one. The incident was a clear case of Dressen floating a smoke-screen to obscure his real intention of getting Marichal to alter his motion.

Later Dressen pulled out a rule book and read aloud from it while conducting demonstrations in the clubhouse. He used a towel as a stand-in for the rubber and kept insisting that Marichal was breaking the rules. Giants manager Tom Sheehan said Dressen was just trying to blow Marichal's concentration. Marichal admitted he was doing exactly what Dressen said he was doing with the placement of his feet, but no one had ever challenged it before.

Marichal felt that his foot positioning aided his curveball delivery, especially to right-handed batters, but he also said that he was unfazed by Dressen's histrionics and was focused on just sticking with the team. "I just pitch my best," Marichal said. "I want to stay up here."

Once the Dressen protest was disposed of, other teams left Marichal alone. And he did stick in the majors.

Such challenges were a sign that Marichal was earning respect among the National League's top players and strategists, who marveled at his skill and his confounding delivery, whether it was the high kick or his variety of pitches.

"He has at least a dozen different deliveries," said Phillies manager Gene Mauch. "The most remarkable thing about Juan is his accuracy. I don't believe I have ever seen a pitcher quite like him."

Hank Aaron, who would hit 755 home runs to set a record that lasted 30 years, was bothered by the Marichal kick.

"His foot is up in your face and that's bad," said Aaron. "With all that confusion of motion, it's a problem seeing the ball. But his control is his biggest asset. He can throw all day and hit a space no wider than two inches, in, out, up, or down."

But for all the talk about the kick, most agreed that Marichal was simply an outstanding pitcher.

Steve Stone, an American League Cy Young Award winner and later a notable broadcaster, was one of those observers.

"If his control wasn't great," Stone said of Marichal, "the leg kick would have been useless. It might have helped with his deception, but the overwhelming stuff and control were what set him apart."

Marichal was not a strikeout specialist. Sandy Koufax set strikeout records. Marichal set efficiency records. Koufax was a power pitcher. Marichal was a sneaky pitcher. Koufax blew batters away with fastballs. Marichal fooled them with fast stuff and slow stuff. Marichal talked about putting the ball where he wanted to when he wanted. It was like the old real estate mantra: location, location, location.

Teammate and pal Felipe Alou said it was nice that Marichal gave credit to his brother Gonzalo for teaching him all that he knew about pitching, but Alou believed Marichal was downplaying his own gift.

"Some of the stuff I saw then, and later on, nobody can teach that," Alou said. "Nobody. That's God-given intelligence, balance, control, toughness. He had everything."

As soon as I began pitching overhand, I loved the style. It worked for me. I tried to learn more every day and perfect my balance. Pitching sidearm is definitely not the same as pitching overhand and kicking your leg so high. It's completely different.

This was the new me. My Springfield manager, Andy Gilbert, accepted my high leg kick even if it was different than what most pitchers did, but as soon as I got to the major leagues the coaches tried to get me to not kick so high.

Sam Jones was a pitcher with the Giants when I first came up to the team. They called him the "toothpick guy" because he always had one in his mouth. He heard the pitching coach talking to me and trying to undermine my pitching style, the height of my throwing, my kicking, and giving me all kinds of reasons why he wanted me to stop the high leg kick. He said they wanted me to stop kicking because I couldn't see the plate if I leaned back so far. I know it seemed as if I was looking at the sky, but how could I be throwing strikes if I was not looking at the plate?

You might throw one strike like that, but not consistently. Right there I threw seven strikes out of 10 pitches. I said, "How can I do that? Do you see how many walks I give up every year? In 200, 300 innings, I give up 70 walks." My control was great.

Sam Jones listened to some of this conversation and told me, "Listen, whatever those guys tell you, let it go through one ear and out the other ear. Don't listen to what they say. Keep pitching the way you do." He was telling me to never let the coaches change me.

Control was really the bottom line of everything I achieved in pitching. Greg Maddux is the best control pitcher in recent years.

Nobody thought of him as a strikeout pitcher, but he struck out a lot of guys because he had such good control.

Everyone who starts to pitch has a fastball first, however fast it is. When you start out as a kid, you throw a fastball because you throw as hard as you can. That's the only thing you know. You might only have a fastball and a slow pitch. I never had a radar gun on my fastball, so I don't know how fast I threw. I don't think I threw hard, but I always had control. Seven out of eight times I could put the ball where I wanted. That was a given. That was a gift, I think. That was the natural ability I had, and I worked on it.

A lot of young guys, when they first come to the majors, try to strike people out with their fastballs. Their fastballs are so good they hardly use anything else. But pitchers get older and they lose speed from their fastballs.

Pedro Martinez was a strikeout pitcher. When he went out to the mound he meant business. Then he had a little arm problem and a sportswriter asked me about him. I said that Pedro had to learn to get guys out without striking out so many. Another sportswriter read that and said, "How can Juan say those things?" That guy criticized me so badly. It was like I was betraying Pedro. I enjoy Pedro a lot and I really love his style. He is not a big guy, but he has a big fastball and he has a big heart. But as all pitchers get older, they can't count on their fastballs as much.

It's not just about striking people out. It is very important to emphasize control.

You might have men on first and third with one out. The first thing you have to think about is making them hit a ground ball for a double play. Only after that can you think about a strikeout. If you strike out the batter, now you have two outs. Now it's a different game because a fly ball to the outfield is the end of the inning. When there is only one out with two men on it can be critical to get a strikeout. And when you are 12 years old, that is a thrill. It's always a thrill, especially when you strike out the last guy of the inning.

The most satisfaction you get as a pitcher is when you strike the batter out after you prepared him. You throw here. You throw there. But you don't want to show him the pitch that you want to get him out on. Then when you do, you strike him out. Oh, my God, I love that feeling.

That's what it's all about, going against the batter like a chess game. That's what I enjoy. When I go and see a baseball game and see a good pitcher, I enjoy watching him do that. I like that guy Cliff Lee, who was with Texas and now is back with the Phillies; he sets up the hitter so well. When Pedro Martinez was in his prime, he was the best.

You enjoy a game when you see those things happen, pitchers setting up the hitters. That's what happens in a baseball game that you don't see in the box score.

When I had good location, good control, I had a lot of confidence. Sometimes you have confidence and then you are accurate. But you have to have a reason to have confidence, confidence and relaxation. When you relax, I think most things come naturally. When I talk to kids about pitching I tell them, "Don't let a guy at the plate intimidate you, no matter how big he is or how strong he looks. You control the ball. You don't throw the ball to the batter. You throw the ball to the catcher. You are trying to keep it away from the batter."

If you relax, you can do whatever you want on the mound. If you're tense, there's no way you can have good mechanics.

The best thing that happened after I mastered throwing overhand was that I learned three different pitches. Throwing sidearm I had just a fastball and a curve. I added the screwball, but with my new delivery I actually had more pitches almost automatically, since I could switch between sidearm and overhand. A fastball alone I could throw overhand, three-quarters, or sidearm. I could throw the curve so that it dropped the right way. I could throw a three-quarters curve and I could throw a sidearm curve. That was really six pitches.

Then I learned the change-up overhand. I could throw that from different spots, too. The sidearm change-up was great against right-handed batters.

But the pitch that I feel kept me at the major-league level for 16 years was my screwball. There is no way you can throw it if you don't know how to control it.

During my time in Springfield I kept hearing about a pitcher named Ruben Gomez, from Puerto Rico, throwing the screwball. Over and over I heard how he had the best screwball in baseball since Carl Hubbell, the old Giants star.

One day I went to my manager, Andy Gilbert, and said that I kept hearing about how great this Ruben was throwing a screwball. I asked, "How do you throw a screwball?"

You throw a screwball the opposite way that you throw a curve-ball—you break your wrist the other way—but you can't throw a screwball sidearm. The motion doesn't work. I had to throw overhand if I wanted to throw a screwball, so I started working on it. Every time I went out on the field to play catch I practiced throwing a screwball. It did not take me long to learn the screwball. I started to use it in games. After I learned that pitch, I threw so many of them.

My screwball became my breaking ball. Once in a while during a season, though, you can lose your ability to throw the screwball. I don't know why—if you lose your grip, or what happens—but for a while it wouldn't work the way I wanted. Because I had so many different pitches, I didn't throw the screwball too often until I got it back. When my screwball worked it used to dance in the air or break so beautifully, especially against the left-handed batter. When they saw the ball it looked like a fastball coming. By the time they got ready to swing, the ball started breaking, and even if they hit it they didn't hit it with much power.

The ball broke away from left-handed hitters, so it was coming in backward for them. They got very frustrated trying to hit.

When I was on the National League all-star team in 1967, I used it to strike out Boston's Carl Yastrzemski, who won the Triple Crown that year. First I showed Carl my fastball in a spot where he couldn't hit it. I didn't want him to even swing at it. I just wanted to show it to him because I was working up to getting him out with a screwball. I got him so bad with the screwball. I struck him out.

The other player that I hurt badly with the screwball, so many times that I feel bad about it, was Bernie Carbo, who was with Cincinnati. One day Orlando came over to the mound from first base because he figured there was just no way I could keep getting Bernie Carbo out with the screwball. Orlando said, "Juan, throw another thing. Throw something else." I laughed and said, "No, he has to learn to hit that one." Carbo got so mad at me he wouldn't talk to me.

It's not that hard to learn the screwball. I think it's easier than the split-fingered fastball. Not that many pitchers try the screwball. They love the split-fingered fastball and I understand that pitch really hurts your arm. Everyone said the screwball hurts the arm, but now, these days, so many pitchers have thumb joint surgery and rotator cuff surgery. I think it's because of the split-fingered fastball.

A lot of people said the screwball was bad for your arm because it has a different torque. Carl Hubbell had thrown so many screwballs that when he retired after 16 seasons in the majors, he couldn't even straighten out his pitching arm. A lot of times he would walk around with his hand in his pocket so it wouldn't show so much.

I think when you throw your screwball from the elbow down to the wrist, you stretch and stress your arm. I learned the pitch by throwing from my shoulder to my elbow and my wrist. I just started it that way. I threw it with the whole arm, not just the bottom half of the arm. Maybe Carl Hubbell didn't know how.

Carl Hubbell was the most famous screwball pitcher of all time, but I knew the screwball and he didn't say much of anything to me about it when I was starting out with the Giants. He didn't say too much at all. He didn't talk to me about his screwball. I read about it and learned he was a great pitcher.

When I was still throwing sidearm, I threw the curveball. I think I pretty much learned that myself. My brother used to have a great moving fastball that was very difficult to hit. But one time he was pitching and the batter hit a line drive that hit him right in the middle of his body. It broke his belt buckle. When I saw that happen I thought, "Oh, my God, I better learn something more about pitching."

When I switched to an overhand delivery, I could throw an overhand curve and a three-quarters curve, plus the sidearm. What made me such a good pitcher later is that I had perfected so many ways of doing things. I could throw any pitch at any time and at any count because my control was so great. It could be my screwball. It could be my slider. Whatever.

I started to get a little bit more interested in the slider after the 1962 World Series. I had seen Jack Sanford throw it all the way from spring training, through the regular season, and in the World Series. His best pitch was the slider. I watched him many times and it got me interested. I learned that pitch and got more confidence about where and when to throw it. I developed it pretty well, but not like Jack.

When Bob Shaw came to the Giants in a trade for Felipe Alou in 1963, he tried to teach Gaylord Perry and me the spitter. One day in Pittsburgh we all went out to the bullpen. We were practicing putting our saliva on the ball, even though it was illegal. After that session, my elbow hurt for the only time in my life, and I never tried it again.

Now Gaylord, well, he became famous for throwing a spitter even though he always said he didn't. He later switched from saliva to Vaseline. He became an expert, the best. Gaylord Perry and I were like brothers. I love him and I'm pretty sure he loves me.

Without all of those pitches there was no way I could have survived against so many left-handed hitters in the major leagues. One time, Gene Mauch, the manager of the Phillies, played nine left-handed batters in the order against me.

From the time I began pitching overhand, kicking my leg high was a natural part of the delivery for me. I was uncomfortable trying to throw overhand without kicking my leg. I don't know if it would have worked if I had been throwing overhand first and then tried to develop the kick. I started kicking the same time I learned to throw overhand.

Let me tell you, I knew right away that I needed good balance to kick like that. If you don't have balance, there's no way you can pitch a strike. No way. You would be throwing the ball all over the place.

I had to work on developing a good mechanics base. Every time I kicked my leg, I learned how to get better balance. Sometimes, in my hotel room, I would stand in front of the mirror and kick my leg. Sometimes I just stood on one foot to see how long I could do that. If you can do that, you learn good balance.

I don't know if there has been anyone else in baseball history that kicked like me. Warren Spahn had a pretty big kick. "El Duque," the pitcher from Cuba—Orlando Hernandez—kicks, but his motion is different. He brings his knee up to his chin with his leg bent. He doesn't kick his leg straight out. I have paintings and photographs of me pitching. Some are more accurate than others. One shows the real way I kicked, way over my head. My glove is down by my ankle. I used to hit my leg with my glove.

When I first saw a picture of myself kicking, I loved it. I can't say that the batters loved it. It looked as if I was kicking at them. It would be confusing for a batter, I think. They are trying to see the ball coming out of my hand and instead they see my foot. That was not on purpose, but the way I had to pitch overhand.

One time in the minors, after I had started to pitch overhand, I kicked my leg so high I ripped my pants. I ripped them right between the legs at the top. That day it was a good thing I knew how to pitch sidearm. I changed back to sidearm right in the middle of the inning and the catcher came out to talk to me. He said, "Hey, what happened? Why don't you throw your regular fastball?" I looked at him and said, "I'll let you know later." When the inning was over I went into the clubhouse to change my pants, and that's when I let the catcher know what happened.

In 1962, when I started the fourth game of the World Series against the Yankees in New York, I struck out Mickey Mantle twice.

In the newspapers, the *New York Times*, the *New York Post*, the next day they interviewed Mickey Mantle and asked him if he was having problems following my pitches. He said, "Well, you know, every time I face that man, the first thing I see is the leg go up and then he looks like he's going to throw the glove at you. The last thing you see is the ball and it's too late to swing at it." That made me feel good coming from Mickey Mantle, one of the best hitters in baseball.

At the end of the season in Springfield, I worked on my overhand pitching. Then I went back to the Dominican to play winter ball for Escogido. This was the first time the people at home had seen me throw anything but sidearm for a long time. This was not the same Juan Marichal they saw leave home in the spring. I was a different person to them. I was throwing with the kick, some sidearm, overhand, throwing all different ways. People started talking about it right away, about the variety of what I was doing.

A lot of people, talking to my friends, to my family, were saying things like, "You have to go and see this guy pitch." It seemed like I was throwing all over the place, and guys at the stadium may not have seen me before and that's the kind of thing they said. "This guy is something. He throws from all over."

The people who knew me said that I was now a different pitcher: "He used to just throw sidearm. Now he throws from here, there and there." Mostly the sportswriters talked about my style and wrote about it a lot. I surprised my friends a lot, too.

Now that I have all the experience, I always tell young people, "You can never tell in baseball." Every day you go to a baseball game you learn something new. Look at me, how I learned to pitch. I was throwing sidearm with two pitches and then I had about 10 pitches.

CHAPTER 7

Duel at 60 Feet, Six Inches

In 1963, Marichal achieved the breakthrough from solid starting pitcher to superstar starting pitcher. He went 25–8, leading the league in wins, with a 2.41 earned run average and a league-high 321⅓ innings. He also had a career-best 248 strikeouts. It was a virtuoso performance.

On June 15, 1963, Marichal recorded one of his biggest thrills as a big-leaguer when he pitched a no-hitter against the Houston Colt .45s at Candlestick Park, striking out 12 batters while throwing just 89 pitches. He became the first Giants pitcher since legendary screwballer Carl Hubbell in 1929 to achieve the feat. He was also the first Latin-born pitcher to throw a no-hitter in the major leagues.

It is hard to argue that the greatest game of a pitcher's career was not *his no-hitter, but Juan Marichal has such a game on his résumé that at least must be considered on the same level of greatness, and it came less than three weeks later.*

On July 2, 1963, Marichal and Milwaukee Braves ace Warren Spahn—a 13-time 20-game winner—hooked up in an epic pitching duel that echoes in baseball annals.

When Marichal walked out to the mound that day at Candlestick Park, there was little reason to think anything special was about to unfold. The Braves were in sixth place in the National League; the Giants were in third. Although Spahn, who later retired as the winningest left-handed pitcher of all time with 363 victories, was 11–3 at the time and Marichal was 12–3, paid attendance was only 15,921.

In a game that lasted four hours and 10 minutes, Marichal and Spahn pitched a double shutout into the 16th inning. They went one-on-one, with no relief pitchers. Several times their managers questioned them about their fatigue levels, and both pitchers said to leave them alone and let them stay in the game.

It was the type of game rarely seen in baseball history, and with the rise of relief pitchers since the 1960s, it has become extinct.

After three innings, each team had recorded a single base hit. In the fourth inning, with two on and two out, Milwaukee's Norm Larker was thrown out at the plate on a single by Del Crandall, ending a Braves rally. The first extra-base hit came off the bat of Spahn, who doubled off Marichal with two out in the seventh. At one point,

Marichal retired 16 batters in a row, and from the ninth inning on, no Braves batter advanced past first base.

Finally, in the bottom of the 16th, the Giants' second batter of the inning, Willie Mays, hit a solo home run to left to win the game.

In the marathon game, Spahn gave up nine hits and one earned run in 15⅓ innings while striking out two and walking one. Marichal gave up eight hits and no runs in 16 innings while striking out 10 and walking four.

Once again, Marichal had followed Hubbell into the Giants' record books. His 16-inning complete game was the longest such performance since Hubbell pitched 18 innings to beat the St. Louis Cardinals 30 years earlier. However, Hubbell did not have a companion matching him inning for inning as Marichal did.

Marichal thought that he and Spahn had nothing particular in common when they pitched, except that Spahn, like Marichal, had a very high leg kick. "Nobody kicks his leg higher than me," Marichal said during the summer of 1963. "Then I see Warren Spahn pitch. He does just like me."

Of course, Spahn had been kicking for a while and was a southpaw, but Marichal got higher lift. Hitters were probably sick of both of them waving a foot in their faces.

AFTER WE MADE IT TO THE WORLD SERIES IN 1962, WE EXPECTED TO GO BACK EVERY YEAR. WE DID WELL DURING THE FIRST part of 1963 but did not do as well in the second half and finished in third place. But I had two of the best pitching performances of my career that year.

On June 15, I pitched a no-hitter against Houston. The funny thing is, I didn't have my good stuff that day. I had nothing on the ball. I did not have good velocity. This was one day when my control was the most important thing. I was hitting my spots with curves and sliders and the batters weren't getting a good piece of the ball. I felt like I was winning the game with a lot of junk. For a while I didn't think about pitching a no-hitter, either. I was working so hard to make the right pitches. I just thought those guys would get a hit.

When I came out for the sixth inning I looked at the scoreboard and realized I still had a no-hitter going and I changed my approach. I went back to throwing my fastball and it began working better. I looked at all those zeroes. Ed Bailey was calling the game behind the plate and I told him I wanted to try some more fastballs.

Through seven innings I had hardly any strikeouts for the game, but I started throwing harder. I don't know where that fastball came from. In the last couple of innings I threw pretty much only the fastball and struck out four batters. I loved pitching that no-hitter, but the thing is I can't understand where that fastball came from, when in those early innings I had nothing.

Usually when Bailey was catching, he would be so friendly and make so many jokes. He would make you laugh. That's what you need on the mound to help you relax. But not that day. That day he did not tell many jokes. All your teammates are superstitious and they don't talk about you pitching a no-hitter.

It was a close game, a real pitcher's duel. The pitcher for Houston was Dick Drott and he gave up only three hits—to Chuck Hiller, Willie Mays, and Jim Davenport. We won only 1–0. We got the only run in the eighth inning, so it was tight all the way.

Houston had only one really hard-hit ball that was close to a base hit. Willie McCovey was in left field that day, which was not his best position, but we had Cepeda playing first base. Carl Warwick, Houston's right fielder, hit a pitch off me that flew to the fence and was about to go over the wall. McCovey was so close to the fence that all he had to do was lift up his arm to catch the ball. That was a home run ball, and Willie saved my no-hitter and shutout.

When the game ended, everyone on the team ran out to me on the mound. They hugged me and rubbed my head and messed up my hair.

One funny story of that no-hitter is that my wife, Alma, was not at the game. She and Felipe's wife were out shopping in San Francisco and they went in a store. Maria, Felipe's wife, saw the screen and said to my wife, "Alma, I think Juan has done something big because I hear a lot of noise. I don't know what it is, but I hear people talking." I don't know whether the people were listening to the TV or radio or something. Then they found out I had a no-hitter.

I forgave her for missing the game. Alma didn't like to come and watch me pitch because she got so nervous. When we started to have kids and the kids got old enough, they wanted to come to the ballpark and see Daddy, so she had to bring them. She used to get so nervous, but I don't know why.

I think every pitcher likes to have a no-hitter on his record. It is always going to be one of a pitcher's favorite games. But that may not have been my best game. About three weeks later I pitched a 16-inning, complete-game win against Warren Spahn and the Braves.

A lot of people ask me about that game. One thing they ask is how many pitches I threw. I threw 227 pitches. When I say that, people can't believe it. That is unheard of in baseball today.

Sixteen innings, and we were both still out there throwing. I was going to stay on the mound as long as they let me. After a while it seems impossible for you to come out until it is finished. I felt good, though. I felt strong. It was not a problem for me. I could have gone a little further. I was a little bit tired afterwards.

When I had my good control, I threw complete games with fewer than 100 pitches. One time I beat the Dodgers in Chavez Ravine with 78 pitches. It was a shutout and the game was over in one hour and 35 minutes.

Whenever I pitched nine innings, a complete game, I felt fine. I could go back out and pitch some more the next day, although not nine innings. But it was the second day after pitching when my arm hurt. I could barely lift it to comb my hair. It was terrible. It would ache all over all the time if I had pitched a long game. So the second day I used to go to the bullpen and just throw a little to loosen up my arm. I let the circulation work. Then the next day I would do a little running and the fourth day I was on the mound again.

My arm was always okay. I never had a sore arm. The only time I felt something that worried me was when I fooled around with throwing the spitter. I threw it a couple of times and my elbow hurt and I quit right away.

One reason baseball is so great is that you always see things you don't expect or you never saw happen before. The day Warren Spahn and I pitched 16 innings, nobody expected that. We didn't expect it, and we didn't even really expect it while it was going on.

There was a play in the ninth inning when Willie McCovey hit a deep fly ball that soared over the foul pole in right field and was called a foul ball. It was straight down the right-field foul line. The umpires called it a foul ball, but I didn't think it was foul. The ball curved, and you could see it land on the foul side, but when the ball left the park I thought it was fair.

First base umpire Chris Pelekoudas made the call that it was foul, but the Giants definitely thought it should have been a home run. Willie thought it was fair. Had it been called that way, the game would have been over in the ninth inning. The managers came out and argued, but the umpire called it foul and it stayed foul. Willie grounded out to first base, and the game went seven more innings.

There have been 16-inning games since then and longer, but not with just two pitchers. I think people remember that game more than my no-hitter.

I didn't know I was going to last 16 innings, of course. No one did. About the ninth inning Alvin Dark came out to the mound and wanted to take me out of the game. I refused. I said I was fine and I told him to look at the Braves dugout and look at Warren Spahn, who was still pitching. Spahn was 42 years old that season. I told Dark, "I am not going to come out of that game as long as that old man is still pitching." I was 25. So he left me in.

I begged him to let me stay in two more innings. In the 12th inning he came back out to the mound and said, "I think you've had enough." Warren Spahn was still pitching, so I said, "Let me stay a few more innings." Every inning he made like he was going to take me out. "Please, Alvin, I feel strong. Let me stay a few more." If Warren Spahn had left the game, maybe I would have, too. But he stayed in and kept pitching. In the dugout after the 14th inning, Dark said, "Keep working."

When I went out to pitch the 15th inning I got worried for a minute about my strength and I said, "Okay, Alvin get somebody ready." I wasn't sure how I would be and thought I might finally need help from the bullpen. But I got them 1-2-3, just like that. Now we have a guy ready to come in after Warren gets our guys 1-2-3 in the bottom of the 15th. I looked to the bullpen and saw our guy start to come in. I grabbed my glove, put my cap on, and ran to the mound. For a minute, I thought there might be two pitchers there for us. I think it was Lindy McDaniel who was getting ready to come in.

I took over the mound and he didn't come in from the bullpen. I got the Braves pretty fast again. Coming back to the dugout I stopped around first base and waited for Willie Mays to come in from center field. When he got near me I put my arm over his shoulder and said, "Alvin's mad at me. I don't think I'm going to be pitching any longer." He touched my back and said, "Don't worry, I'm going to win this game for you."

I knew Alvin was mad at me for going back out there, but the entire game catcher Ed Bailey said, "Don't let them take you out."

So Willie comes up in the bottom of the 16th inning and hits a home run over the left-field wall. Oh, what a relief. By winning that game I knew Alvin couldn't really say anything. I just didn't want to leave my game. What a game.

One thing I don't understand about this modern era of pitching is how starters never throw complete games, even just nine innings. They go out to the mound and pitch six innings and call it a "quality start." I didn't like to come out of my games. People are amazed when I tell them I won 243 games and pitched 244 complete games in my career. I had 18 complete games in 1963, 22 in 1964, 24 in 1965, 25 in 1966, and would you believe that in 1968 I had 30 complete games? That was our job.

The only time I asked to come out of a game was one time when I was struggling and felt really bad. The manager came out to the mound to talk to me. I said, "I don't feel good." He said to me, "Turn around and look over there." He pointed to the bullpen. I said, "I see two guys warming up there." He said, "Well, you said you feel bad, right?" I said, "Yes, real bad." He said, "Well, the way you feel, you are still much better than the guys there."

So I stayed in the game and I finished the game so strong. I couldn't believe it. I couldn't believe how I felt after he gave me that confidence. It was pretty funny the way he said it, though.

Every game I started, I was prepared for nine innings. I didn't think about the bullpen or relief pitchers. In 1961, my record was 13–10, but at one time during the season it was 6–6 and every pitch was a struggle. You just have bad streaks sometimes. The whole team was pitching badly. Everybody. So Alvin came up with a rule for us. He said, "No bullpen." He didn't even put the relief pitchers out there the first game. They were in the dugout. And you know what happened? I pitched seven straight wins with the "No bullpen" rule.

Can you believe the closer in today's game? He comes out and let's say he makes one pitch. He gets credit for the save. And those guys get a ton of money. Of course, everybody makes a ton of money compared to when I pitched—holy cow. The most money I made in a season was $140,000 in 1972. I made $24,000 in 1963 when I had that great year, and that got me a raise to $40,000.

When I pitched, you were supposed to go nine innings once the manager gave you the ball. Maybe if I pitched in today's era, I would feel the same way as these guys today—pitch six or seven innings and that's enough, save my arm. I could still make a lot of money because you don't have to pitch nine innings to make good money.

We also started every fourth day, not every fifth day. All my career I did that. Now when they announce that someone is going to pitch on three days' rest, they make a big deal out of that. Like, "Can he do it?" I did it for 16 years.

The relief pitchers, the closers, have learned how to pitch every day. It is only one inning, or one batter, whatever, and sometimes they warm up and they don't have to come in. So why can't starting pitchers learn how to go nine innings? You have to get your arm strong and your legs. Your legs have to get a lot of exercise. In my day, they didn't have all the fancy equipment they have now for exercise. You ran. You ran all the time. You didn't see that many players hurt. Maybe they don't know how to use those machines and that's why so many guys get hurt now.

Warren and I did not speak after our big 16-inning battle, but the next day Alvin went to the Braves side and asked if Warren, as an experienced pitcher, would talk to me about how to take care of my arm after a game like that. Warren and I went out into right field and talked for a little while and he showed me some exercises I could do before my next game. I couldn't forget what Warren told me. That was so nice of him, considering he was the losing pitcher. In my house, I have a photo of Warren and me together.

Many years later, Warren and I were both in Cooperstown, New York, at one of the events they hold before new members get inducted into the Hall of Fame. He told us that every late inning during our 16-inning game, his manager talked to him and wanted to take him out. He told his manager that he wasn't coming out of the game until that young kid pitching on the other side came out. I laughed so hard when I heard that story.

I liked Warren as a pitcher and a human being. We got so close from visits in Cooperstown. I brought my son, Juanchi, with me that year, and Warren invited my son to visit his ranch. He wanted to take him home with him, but Juanchi was still in school. I think he was about 16, so he couldn't go to the ranch.

Warren Spahn was such a great pitcher. He won 23 games that year at age 42. He was a winner. I saw him win a game 8–7. He gave up something like five home runs that game, but he refused to give up. That shows that you can't let home runs discourage you. It is really hard to do, but you have to forget about it right away.

Sometimes a ball is hit right down the foul line and, from the mound, you try to push that ball foul with your mind. But when it's a home run, you can't dwell on it at all. You have about 30 seconds to get your concentration back before the next guy comes to the plate. You might end up walking that guy, and if it's a guy like Maury Wills or Lou Brock, he might steal second on you right away. You might have thrown a bad pitch to give up the home run, but that is not the time to worry about it. You have to give the hitter some credit sometimes, too.

Spahn gave up a lot of home runs in his career, but he always kept battling as long as he was in the game. You can watch some pitchers in baseball and they seem to have the best stuff, but they might not be winners. They pitch a good game, but they find a way to lose. Warren was a different type of pitcher. He found a way to win.

He was a tough player, and he was a pretty good hitter, too. Now that he has passed away, I miss him. He was a fun guy to be around. He was the kind of guy who made you laugh. And he was a great, great pitcher.

CHAPTER 8

Latins Find a Home in the Majors

*I*n the same way that Major League Baseball ignored generations of American-born black ballplayers with an unwritten but very real ban that consigned them to the shadows of the sport for the first half of the 20th century, dark-skinned Latin American players were also kept on the outside.

An institution that could pretend that Satchel Paige, Cool Papa Bell, Josh Gibson, Buck Leonard, Judy Johnson, Oscar Charleston, and many others were not worthy of a place on a major league roster found it no more difficult to exclude the finest Latin players, such as Martin Dihigo, Cristobal Torriente, and others.

Even today Martin Dihigo is not nearly as famous as Satchel Paige and Josh Gibson, but some believe he was the greatest baseball player of all time. The Cuban-born Dihigo, who broke into Latin baseball as a 16-year-old in 1922 and played for more than two decades before becoming a manager, was an all-star in the Negro Leagues and is in the Baseball Hall of Fame in Cooperstown, as well as in the halls of fame of Cuba, Mexico, the Dominican, and Venezuela.

One year in Mexico, Dihigo went 18–2 as a pitcher with a 0.90 earned run average and led the Mexican League in hitting at .387.

At one point after he retired, Juan Marichal participated in a Hall of Fame fantasy camp organized by Roy Campanella, the great Dodgers catcher. Marichal asked Campanella who was the best player he ever saw. "He said he didn't know how to pronounce the name correctly," Marichal recounted, "but it was Martin Dihigo. He was the best player he ever saw."

Because of his dark skin, though, Dihigo was never welcome in the majors.

The exceptions to the discrimination against Latinos were players who were deemed sufficiently light-skinned. Cuba, the Dominican Republic, Puerto Rico, Mexico, and even Nicaragua were hotbeds of baseball even before the dawn of the 20th century. Nowhere was the game more beloved and developed in Latin America than in Cuba, and the first Latin American star in the majors emerged from that island nation.

Adolfo Luque, who was born in 1880, was blue-eyed and light-skinned, so by baseball's definition he classified as "white." Luque made his major league debut with the Boston Braves in 1914. He became a solid right-hander, at times touching stardom, primarily for the Cincinnati Reds in a career that extended until 1935. In 1923, Luque led the National League in wins with 27 and in earned run average with a tremendous mark of 1.93. He also led the NL in ERA in 1927 and won 194 games in his major league career.

Luque was later the pitching coach for the New York Giants and managed in Cuba. He was known as short-tempered, perhaps contributing to the American stereotype of Latinos as being prone to hotheadedness. His first language was Spanish, and he spoke English with an accent.

Few other Latin ballplayers made their mark until the 1950s, primarily because many of them were dark-skinned and not welcome until after Jackie Robinson broke the color barrier when he suited up for the Brooklyn Dodgers in 1947. Once teams accepted American blacks, they began scouting players in Latin America.

Minnie Minoso, a Cuban who was a hero to many early Latin players, was considered the first black player for the Chicago White Sox when he broke in during the 1951 season, although the White Sox already had light-skinned Venezuelan Chico Carrasquel at shortstop. Dominican Ozzie Virgil Sr. played a couple of seasons with the Giants in the 1950s before becoming the first black player for the Detroit Tigers.

More than a decade passed with dark-skinned Latin players being invited into the majors before Juan Marichal joined the Giants in 1960. Players such as Vic Power, Roberto Clemente, Luis Aparicio, and Felipe Alou preceded him. But Latin players who came up in the late 1950s and early 1960s still had much to overcome. The location and degree of tolerance in the team's home cities, and how well the player adapted to the English language, dictated the depth of challenge he faced.

The arrival of Latin American players in the majors could be measured as a trickle when Marichal became a Giant. He was one of only a handful of Dominicans at the top of the sport and the first great pitcher from his country to make it big.

When I came up to the majors in 1960, there were still not very many Latin players in the league, but they were starting to make a difference. Roberto Clemente was established as a star with the Pirates. Vic Power was with the Indians at that time. Felipe Alou. Luis Aparicio. Chico Carrasquel. Orlando Cepeda. Orlando got big right away. He was the National League Rookie of the Year in 1958.

I knew that times were changing. Things had been improving over the years. There were better opportunities for Latin players, and I was one of those to take advantage of that opportunity. I always say that getting into the major leagues was easy, but the hard thing was staying at the major league level. Back then you knew everyone in the majors who was from a Latin American country. They weren't all Dominican, but we had a bond together because we shared a common background and language. But there were not so many that you couldn't keep track of them.

Some Latin players had gone to the United States to play, but they were confronted by some of the racial problems of the time. Some were given just a very brief opportunity to become a major leaguer and then went home. I think the organizations should have had more patience with some of those players and worked with them. I think there were unspoken rules about how many Latin players a team could have, and so not everyone had the same opportunity to make the team. I think they had a quota.

That's what comes to my mind, because when you talk about the people who went to the United States and came back, some of them could have been great players. They were never given a real opportunity.

I had a lot of respect for Clemente. They wanted to call him Bob when he came to the United States to play baseball. Some of the sportswriters called him Bob. He always said to call him Roberto. He was very proud of being Hispanic.

We were already in the major leagues when I first met him. He was about five years ahead of me when he joined the Pittsburgh Pirates, so he was established when I was a rookie. You knew right away that he was a winner because of how he played. If he hit it back to the mound, you had to hurry or he would beat the throw to first base.

He never quit. He never gave up. That's how the game should be played. I love to see players hustle like that. Roberto Clemente became a king or an idol for all Latin American players, not just those from his native Puerto Rico. He was a great player and he was very proud. He was a role model, a leader for all Latin players.

Part of it was his timing, because there had not been many Latin stars when he came into the league. But there had been others, and you didn't see other young players from different countries try to be like them. Clemente surpassed the borders of ball-playing with the way he played the game.

If you just watched him play, you knew he was a leader. That's why so many players tried to follow his style, and Roberto Clemente became an idol to them. For years, many Latin players from all countries wore No. 21 in his honor.

Of course, I had to pitch to him. He did everything well and he won several batting titles. I had to figure out how to get him out. It wasn't easy. Sometimes I would luck out against him. And he was such a great fielder with a powerful arm, too—oh my. At that big old field in Pittsburgh, Forbes Field, he played that wall in right field so well. The ball would hit the concrete wall and the hitter thought he had an easy double. Roberto would turn and throw, and the runner had to go back to first base and hope he didn't get thrown out there.

At that time, in the 1960s, the Giants and the Pirates had the most Latin players and we all knew each other. We would get together in the dugouts and talk before the games sometimes. I was the only pitcher and I listened when they talked about hitting.

One time we got to the park very early for a game and a bunch of the Latin players got together to talk. Orlando and Roberto and Jose Pagan and all of those guys were talking and I heard Roberto say that I was the pitcher that gave him the most trouble, and that it was because of my outside fastball. I was not in a groove at that time. I was far from being in a groove.

I was pitching the next day, and when I faced Roberto I threw him nothing but fastballs outside and I struck him out three times. If you know just a little bit about a hitter, it can help you with your game. He got his share of hits off me, too. He got his share against every pitcher. He was a great player and human being.

Baseball named its Humanitarian Award after Roberto, so that should tell you who he was. And the way he died, flying relief supplies to Nicaragua after an earthquake. He just wanted to help people. It was very sad when he died.

Roberto once said he wanted to be a chiropractor. I was having trouble with my back so he used to give me what they call adjustments. I used to go to the clubhouse to get an adjustment from him. One day he told me, "Oh, if the owner of the team sees me doing this, they're going to fire me." But he was a great human being. I was very close with Roberto and Chico Carrasquel and Luis Aparicio.

Vic Power was a very good player. The Yankees would not give him a chance. They told him he couldn't date white women. Vic Power did whatever he wanted, but he was married to a light-skinned Latin woman. The woman people saw him with was his wife! The Yankees got rid of him and he went on to be a star player for the Kansas City Athletics, Cleveland Indians, and Minnesota Twins. Vic Power liked to drive big cars, typically a Cadillac. The Yankees just didn't like his style.

Hector Lopez was the first Latin player the Yankees gave a chance to. They liked him better than Vic.

When you see what happened with Cuba, where Fidel Castro wouldn't let players out of the country and stopped them from playing professionally, you know the Trujillos could have done that to me if they really wanted to keep me playing for the Air Force. But nobody blocked us from going to play baseball in the United States. It certainly could have happened. The Trujillos could have said, "This is what we want. You can't go." And there was nothing I could have done about it.

When I was a kid I used to follow Cuban baseball. That general, Jose Garcia Trujillo, who was Alma's uncle, used to talk about the Cuban ballplayers. My ambition was to make the Dominican national team, but I thought someday I might go to Cuba to play baseball. I thought it would be pretty good to go to Havana. Baseball was the biggest thing in the Caribbean and it was the best in Cuba. But then Fidel took over baseball there. That made it very hard for some of the best Cuban players. Luis Tiant, Tony Perez, Minnie Minoso, and Tony Oliva all had to leave their home country and never go back. They didn't see their parents, or their brothers and sisters, for years.

And there are hundreds of Cuban players over all these years who might have been good enough to play in the United States and make a living to support their families. They grew old playing baseball in Cuba.

When I think about the Cuban players who never had the chance to come to the United States, I get sad. It seems to me the system was so bad, because how can you stop somebody from making a better life for themselves? Any player that came from any Latin country to the United States would have had the chance to make good money. Even when it was only thousands of dollars, that was much more than you would make working a farm. Now the players make millions. That changes your life forever. It can help your family forever.

One guy stops you from being a success—one guy means you are in poverty—because he, Fidel, doesn't want you to go to the United States to play baseball. I think that's wrong. It's been 50 years now. It's unbelievable.

Look around. Look how many players from the Dominican, Venezuela, Mexico, and Puerto Rico have been successful. When Latins first started playing in the majors, Cuba was No. 1. How many guys would have made it from Cuba? All this time they don't let players go from Cuba, and now the Dominican is No. 1. Cuba had so many good players. It's a sad story.

I remember when Luis Tiant was not able to go back to Cuba and his parents were getting old. They finally were allowed to go to the United States to visit him and see him play—Fidel let them go—when Luis was with the Red Sox. But Luis's old friends and relatives in Cuba couldn't see him. That really touched my heart. He could have helped a lot of people there if he had been able to go back.

It was an emotional story when his parents got to visit him in Boston. His father threw out the first pitch at a Red Sox game. Luis was crying. His father had been a very good pitcher in Cuba, but he never got a chance to see his son pitch until then. His folks got to see him before they died.

Orlando Cepeda's father, Perucho, told him not to go to the United States from Puerto Rico because of the racism. Orlando wanted to go, but his father thought he would be hurt by the way things were. It is sad to even have that on your mind. Thankfully, for Orlando it worked out.

I was lucky when I got to the Giants, in 1960, because Felipe Alou was already there and I had known him so long. I lived with Matty as roommates at Mrs. Johnson's in San Francisco. The Alous are all great people. I knew their mother and father, too. Those kids grew up near the ocean in Haina. They loved to fish and play baseball.

Between the three of them, Felipe made it to the highest level in school because he went to university. Matty and Jesus signed very young and played baseball instead.

What a family. I am so close to them. I baptized one of Felipe's daughters and he baptized one of my daughters, my first one. I was the best man at Jesus's wedding. And through the Alous is how I got to know Alma. We have been great, great friends for a long time. It's pretty lucky to have friends like that.

Felipe was a great, great player. He could play every position in the outfield. He had a great arm and was a good hitter. He was smart. He was the kind of player you wanted on your team. If Felipe had a problem it was that he didn't hit more home runs, but that was because he hit so many line drives. He hit the ball so hard down the left-field line that the third base coach had to coach outside the box to stay clear of those liners. Felipe played 17 years in the majors, hit 206 home runs, and batted .286. He made the all-star team three times. Just a great ballplayer. He proved how smart he was when he became a manager later for the Expos and then the Giants.

Felipe came up as an outfielder with the Giants in 1958, so he was already there when I came up from the minors. That was very good for me. He helped me so much to get adjusted.

Matty signed with the Giants, too. He played in San Francisco just a few games during my first year and was with the team until 1965. They just didn't give him the opportunity to play every day. He hit .310 in 1961 but only played in 81 games. He got stuck hitting in the .240s or .260s and they traded him to the Pirates. I was very sad when he left. But right away Pittsburgh saw the potential he had.

The Pirates had a hitting coach named Harry Walker who became the manager, and Walker took Matty and gave him a heavy bat. They used to go the stadium together, and Walker pitched batting practice to Matty. He practiced and practiced, and Walker taught him to hit the ball down, and Matty became a .300 hitter. The first year in Pittsburgh he batted .342 and won the National League batting title, hitting more than 100 points higher than he had in his last year with the Giants. And the following year, 1967, he hit .338 and just missed winning the batting title again.

The third basemen on other teams would always play Matty too far back, so he became an expert at bunting for hits. Sometimes the third baseman would play in and Matty wouldn't bunt. Then the fielder would back up and Matty would bunt on two strikes, which not too many hitters do. He would drop the ball in there and get on base. That would drive the other team crazy. He was something.

I would say Jesus Alou was a natural hitter. He swung like Vladimir Guerrero. Jesus used to swing at everything, but he made contact. Some hitters swing at everything but don't make contact with the ball. But Jesus made contact, somehow, wherever the ball was. One time in San Francisco, Jim Bunning was pitching for the Phillies and he threw a pitch about level with Jesus's head. Jesus swung at it and hit a home run to right field. He was that type of hitter.

Jesus came to the Giants late in the 1963 season and stayed with the team for five years after that. At one point, the Giants had three Alou brothers playing in the outfield at the same time. Jesus was in the major leagues until 1979 and played for two World Series champions in Oakland.

Playing with the Alous on the Giants was lucky for me. Not only did I have other Latin players around to share things with and speak Spanish with, but they were old friends from my home country that I had known most of my life. With the four of us in San Francisco, the Giants were very popular in the Dominican. After that they had other guys to cheer for—Manny Mota for a short time and later a guy named Elias Sosa. That was only the beginning. We started getting a lot of guys who made it. That made the Dominican fans very happy.

Another good thing about being with the Alou brothers was that our wives could be together. Felipe got married first, and then Matty and I got married at almost the same time. All three wives came to San Francisco to live with us. Felipe's wife, Maria, helped Alma a lot. She didn't know how to cook and Maria taught her. Alma became one of the best cooks in the world. They helped each other and gradually became less homesick.

Felipe was the smart one of all of us, and that's why he became a manager. He always knew what he was doing. He had great dignity and wisdom. In the United States they say of this kind of guy, "He has his head on straight." Matty's wife, Teresa, and my wife, Alma, used to tell us to follow Felipe because he was a great man. He is the type of man that when he talks, everybody listens. He gives young players good advice.

The bad thing for us was when the Giants traded Felipe away after the 1963 season. They sent him to the Braves for pitcher Bob Shaw.

It hurt all the Giants' Latin players when Felipe was traded. He was a very good teammate and he was a guide for the Latin players. The way he acted, the way he wanted you to be, and the advice he gave us all was very important. He told you how to act as a big-leaguer and how to play in the field. Felipe was all about being a man. When he got the job as a manager for the Montreal Expos in the minors, he helped so many young kids, and they loved him. Many of those kids became major leaguers, too. They loved to play for Felipe and loved the way he treated them. He even ended up managing his son Moises, in Montreal and later in San Francisco.

When Felipe was traded, we kept asking the team questions. Why did they do it? Why did they trade him? The answer we got was that Felipe wanted to become a religious minister and they were afraid that he would retire and they would lose him and not get anything for him. I don't know if that is a true story, but Felipe was involved with a wonderful person who used to be a minister of a church in California. They were very close. So the team thought Felipe was going to quit baseball and become a minister. But Felipe didn't retire from playing until 1974, more than 10 years later, and then stayed in baseball as a manager.

Orlando Cepeda was not Dominican. He was from Puerto Rico. But he was like a brother to us, too. Everybody liked Orlando. Players had a lot of respect for him. Orlando was more popular in San Francisco than Willie Mays. He came from the farm system and joined the big-league club in 1958 when the Giants started in San Francisco. Willie was already established from the New York days. It was like Orlando belonged more to San Francisco.

We were friends with all types of players on the team, but the Latin players had a special bond, a brotherhood. We had so much in common, even if we were not from the same country. We were from the same part of the world with the same kind of climate. We spoke the same language. We had darker skin and we had experienced discrimination in the United States because of that.

We were spread out, and guys lived in different areas of the city, but we did socialize with each other away from the ballpark, especially when other teams that had a lot of Latin players came to town to play us. Sometimes they would come for four games at a time so they stayed for several days, and we would have the Latin players to dinner. It's not like football or other sports where the team just flies into town, plays a game, and goes home.

We showed the visiting guys some hospitality because we knew it could be lonely on the road as a Latin person in another city. The Pirates had a lot of Latin players, so we always invited them for dinner, and when we went to Pittsburgh they had us over. We ate with Roberto, Manny Sanguillen, Vic Davalillo, and Manny Mota when he was with the Pirates. We went to different houses each time. Chicago was a place that had a lot of Latin residents, so we could go out and have a good time.

The Latin players stuck together when it came to socializing. When Manny Mota went to the Dodgers, we still went to his home and the homes of other Latin players—even if the Dodgers were our chief rivals. Our friendships had nothing to do with the rivalry on the field.

Manny Mota is a great guy, and what a great hitter. He was the best pinch hitter of all time. He kept saying he was going to retire and be a coach. Then, in the middle of the next season, they would put him on the active roster and you would come to town and there would be Manny—hitting again. They kept doing that. He is still with the Dodgers coaching. It has been about 35 years now. I keep thinking one day I will wake up and I will see him batting again.

In the late 1950s and the early part of the 1960s, it was mostly the Giants and Pirates signing Latin players. They had a big jump on most other teams, especially in the National League. They really made an effort, and that's why there were so many Latin players on those clubs. Then the Dodgers jumped in. The Atlanta Braves, too, after a while. They signed Rico Carty, who won a batting championship. And they traded for Felipe.

Some teams didn't have any Latin players during the early period of my career. It took quite a while for things to change. We were small in numbers, but I like to think that we helped open doors for other Latin players who came along, the generations that followed us.

CHAPTER 9

A Lifetime of Regret

*P*eople who know Juan Marichal, or who merely meet him in passing, consider him a friendly man with a big heart whose default facial expression is a smile. He gets along well with almost everyone and can usually find the good in someone.

That is why it is so surprising that one of the most notorious on-field incidents in baseball history is attached to his good name. It seems such an aberration, and people who meet the man cannot believe he is one and the same person who in 1965 was embroiled in a violent confrontation with Los Angeles Dodgers catcher Johnny Roseboro.

Typically, baseball fights involve a lot of milling around, some bear hugs, shouting, or finger-pointing. Rarely do real punches connect and even more rarely is any real harm done. The dust-up between Marichal and

Roseboro on August 22, 1965—a date that Marichal remembers as easily as his birth date—was both more extreme and more memorable for its seriousness than nearly all other brawls. The incident stained Marichal's otherwise impeccable reputation, although time has healed most of the wounds.

On that day, in the intense atmosphere of a game against the rival Dodgers in San Francisco, Marichal swung a bat at Roseboro and hit him in the head. The act enraged Dodger teammates, caused Marichal's expulsion, and drew speculation that he might face criminal charges on top of any discipline meted out by Major League Baseball.

The Giants and Dodgers were keen rivals. Dodgers right-hander Don Drysdale, as was his wont, had sent Willie Mays sprawling to the ground twice in a game earlier that summer and announced that he was "protecting" his hitters. He received a warning from National League President Warren Giles that future high and inside fastballs like that would result in a $1,000 fine.

The August 22 game was the fourth in another series between the teams, and the Dodgers had won two of the first three. The game matched Marichal and Sandy Koufax, the two premier hurlers in the sport.

Emotions were very raw, and not only because of the baseball action. At that time, there was civil unrest in the Dominican Republic, where most of Marichal's family still lived, and the United States had sent the Marines to restore stability. Roseboro, meanwhile, was from the Watts neighborhood of Los Angeles, where major riots had taken place earlier that month over issues of civil rights, police brutality, and other social issues.

During a game earlier in the series, Dodgers shortstop Maury Wills swung at a pitch and tipped catcher Tom Haller's mitt. The umpire ruled interference and awarded Wills first base. Giants manager Herman Franks flew out of the dugout to argue, suggesting that Wills had done the interfering with his bat on purpose. In the bottom of the inning, Matty Alou took a swing in the batter's box and hit Roseboro's mitt. This time the umpire declared that Alou had done so intentionally and refused to give him first base. The Giants bench erupted in protest.

This led to a considerable amount of gamesmanship and trash-talking as the series went on. Marichal was among those yelling at Roseboro and the Dodger players from the dugout. At one point after returning to the dugout, Alou told Marichal that Roseboro said he should shut up or he would get the ball thrown in his ear. There was no bad blood between Marichal and Roseboro previously, so he felt it was just talk from Roseboro.

Earlier in the game, Marichal had thrown a brush-back pitch at Dodgers first baseman Ron Fairly. Koufax, who did not throw at hitters as a matter of personal policy, threw one pitch to Willie Mays that sailed harmlessly over his head. It was at best a token symbol.

Marichal's turn at bat came at the start of the bottom of the third inning, and after a low pitch that Roseboro dropped, the catcher scooped the ball up right behind

Marichal and zinged it back to Koufax. The ball was so close to his head that Marichal said it nicked his ear. Marichal and Roseboro exchanged angry words, and Marichal thought Roseboro was going to attack him the way he stepped up. Quickly assessing that Roseboro was wearing a mask, a chest protector, and shin guards—in essence what the pitcher said was more or less a suit of armor—Marichal realized that he would be at a disadvantage in a fistfight.

Marichal thought Roseboro was going to hit him. So he swung the bat at the top of Roseboro's head. The blow opened a gash on Roseboro's head and blood rushed down his face. Koufax charged in from the mound to separate the players, and Mays rushed out from the bench and ran to Roseboro's aid. A lot of grabbing and shoving ensued between other Dodgers and Giants players in the aftermath.

Roseboro was soon guided off the field. Marichal was thrown out of the game.

The repercussions were severe by 1965 standards. Marichal was suspended for nine days and fined $1,750. Giles issued a strong reprimand of Marichal. In part, it read, "I am sure you recognize how repugnant your actions were in your game at San Francisco. . . . Such actions are harmful to the game, have no place in sports, and must be drastically dealt with."

Although assault charges were not filed, Roseboro did sue Marichal and the Giants for "unprovoked assault" and was awarded $10,000 in civil court. The Giants disputed the "unprovoked assault" claim because Roseboro had said *more than a day prior to the incident that he was going to "get" someone on the Giants.*

The incident became the one serious blemish on Marichal's career. He had never been a troublemaker before and he was never a troublemaker again, but his confrontation with Roseboro followed him forever.

Decades later, a writer-actor named Roger Guenveur Smith penned a play called Juan and John. *Marichal saw a showing along with Roseboro's daughter in 2009 and met the playwright. He considered it a very moving rendition of what transpired during that awful moment at the ballpark and later.*

DURING THIS TIME WHEN I WAS PITCHING SO WELL IN THE MID-1960s, THE GIANTS AND THE DODGERS HAD A BIG RIVALRY. Every game we played seemed huge. It was like it had been back in New York, I was told. We were 400 miles apart, but we were the only two teams on the West Coast at the time, so the rivalry just moved. I didn't know how big it was in New York, but it was unbelievable in California. The rivalry was not only with the players, but the fans, too, and even the cities.

I remember that the fans from San Francisco used to go to Los Angeles to watch the games there. People asked the visitors if they were from "Frisco" and they said, "No, we're from San Francisco." Fans asked if the other side was from "L.A." and they said, "No, Los Angeles." They were very particular about that.

The Dodgers were a very good team. They had Sandy Koufax and Don Drysdale as their top two pitchers, both guys in the Hall of Fame. These were the years in the early 1960s when Sandy was so great. He won 25 or more games three times from 1963 to 1966. Beginning in 1961, he led the National League in strikeouts four times and in earned run average five times. Three of those times he gave up less than two runs a game for a whole season. Whew, that man could pitch.

They had some very good hitters, too, like Tommy Davis, who had 230 hits and batted .346 one year. He was always good against me, until he broke his ankle in 1965. They also had Willie Davis, who was so fast. That guy used to fly with a long stride. You couldn't always tell how fast he was, but he was. They were still playing in the Los Angeles Coliseum in 1960 and 1961 and they had that very short left-field fence that was about 250 feet or something. Outfielder Wally Moon was a right-handed hitter whose home runs over that fence were called "Moon Shots." Every time a ball was hit that way and it didn't go out, it hit the wall and was a double.

Los Angeles also had Jim Gilliam and Maury Wills. And Duke Snider, another Hall of Famer, was still a big hitter. Gil Hodges was still there. He was a big guy with a good swing and a really good first baseman. He had a really good glove. In 1962, Maury Wills set the all-time record for stolen bases with 104, and that lasted for a while until Lou Brock broke it. That guy, you couldn't let him on base. I remember the time Alvin Dark wanted to wet down the base paths with a hose so Wills couldn't steal. I didn't think it was a good idea. But it worked. He couldn't get traction with his spikes. But that's wrong, I think. You don't stop a player's quality by doing that sort of thing. Wills was a real headache for a pitcher. I think he belongs in the Hall of Fame. Gil Hodges, too.

For a while it seemed like I pitched against Sandy Koufax all the time, but I think it was only a few times. After a little while Dark decided not to pitch me against him. You know, Sandy beat me with a no-hitter. That's what would happen, so Alvin stopped putting us head-to-head, figuring I might be able to beat the next guy if we couldn't hit Sandy. But the next guy was Don Drysdale, and he went to the Hall of Fame, too. My peers, my teammates didn't like to play against Drysdale. They would rather bat against Sandy. Drysdale would throw at people. He didn't care. Sandy wouldn't throw at batters. Drysdale was tough. He was the type of pitcher if his mother came to the batter's box and was crowding the plate, he would knock her down. It didn't bother him at all. He would shave the hitters and keep on pitching.

Sandy was so good because he had the best fastball and the best breaking ball, and after a while he became a control pitcher, too.

In the beginning he was so wild, but when he found that control he was very tough, very hard to beat. You didn't want to get into the batter's box against him. When you hit against Sandy, you could hear that fastball passing you. You could hear the wind. One time I was hitting against him and he threw a breaking ball. I saw the ball head high and I started to swing at it and that ball started breaking down, so I followed it. I broke the bat on home plate. I hit down at it using the bat like it was a sledgehammer. Now that's a breaking ball.

It was too bad that he had to retire when he was only 30. I used to talk to him a lot during the All-Star Game, when we were on the same team. One time the game was in St. Louis and it was so hot. They put a thermometer on the field in center field. It went up to something like 152 and it busted. Every time a player came from the outfield to the bench he went to the water fountain and put cold water on his shoes because it was so hot. I think that was the hottest day in my whole career that I had to play.

And that day Sandy Koufax put a heat treatment on his arm. It's the type of thing that burns your skin it's so hot. When I saw him do it that day, I thought, "Man, this guy is hurting." To put that stuff on your arm in that kind of heat, that was unbelievable.

When Sandy announced he was going to retire, it shocked quite a lot of people, but it didn't surprise me because I knew he had problems. I knew he couldn't handle the feeling he got in his arm every time he threw.

The date was August 22, 1965. I wish that it never happened. It was unbelievable that it happened. I don't think I have a temper.

But something really, really blew up in my head. It was the circumstances of the time, and I don't like to talk about what happened, especially since Johnny and I became good friends later in life.

At the very end of my career I signed to play with the Dodgers. It was a strange match because we had been such great rivals. Some people wondered how the fans would like me and how the organization would like me. They still remembered Johnny and me and the bat. But Johnny called the Dodgers and told them to give me a warm welcome and to forget what happened that day, that it was part of the game.

I think that was very nice of him. We became good friends in about 1975, and later I invited him to come to the Dominican and play in the Juan Marichal Golf Tournament that I have each year for charity. He came with his wife, Barbara, and his daughter, and they became good friends with my family and we had a good relationship after that time.

Since he passed away in 2002, I don't like to talk about what happened anymore because I don't want anyone in his family to misunderstand or say anything that they think is not true. I lived with that story inside me for many years.

A couple of years after I was inducted into the Hall of Fame, I was sitting outside the hotel in Cooperstown during one of the annual gatherings and Fergie Jenkins, the Cubs pitcher, came and sat down next to me. He said, "Juan, are you and Johnny friends?" And I said, "Oh yes, we became good friends." Fergie said, "I'm so happy to hear that because I know what happened that day."

Fergie said he knew the way the game was going, with the pitchers throwing warning fastballs, that the Dodgers had to treat our hitters like that and he knew that Sandy never threw at hitters. At the time people knew that Johnny had said, "Let me do it," as a warning to me instead of having Sandy throw at me. That's what Fergie said. Johnny knew that Sandy didn't throw at hitters, and if he did, they might throw him out of the game, and he was too valuable to lose. So Johnny said he would take care of it.

I asked Fergie, "Do you know Sandy?" He knew that Sandy didn't throw at hitters. I felt such a relief knowing that somebody else knew what happened out there, that somebody else knew the whole scene. They had planned the whole thing, and Johnny said, "Leave Juan to me."

I was the bad guy for using a bat, and I know I did wrong for using the bat, but when that ball hit my ear I jumped back and said, "Why did you do that?" He called my mother so many names.

He was very angry and he mentioned my name and my mother's name so many times. I said, "What?" When he charged at me, I didn't know what to do. I wasn't trying to hurt him. I was trying to stop him. Hitting him with a baseball bat was wrong, no question, but I was never trying to hurt him. I was trying to stop him from getting to me. Even though I know I was provoked, that was the worst thing that happened in my career. The worst, I know.

We were yelling and we were angry, but that doesn't mean I should have hit him with the bat. I have to live with that for the rest of my life. People will always bring it up, but I am not as bothered by it anymore because Johnny and I had a good friendship so many years after that. That was the good part of it.

The Giants and Dodgers were such rivals, and people asked me why I went over there to play for Los Angeles at the end of my career. But I was glad I went because I got to know the O'Malley family that owned the team. They treated me as a friend. I can't forget that, so I don't regret going to the Dodgers.

A portrait of me as a pitcher with
Escogido in 1959. I pitched for Escogido
before I went to the big leagues and also
during the offseason early in my career.
Marichal collection

The Giants had five players in the 1962 All-Star Game—Felipe Alou, Jim Davenport,
Willie Mays, me, and Orlando Cepeda—and I earned the win in the game.
Marichal collection

The 1965 All-Star Game had several prominent Latin players, including Felix Mantilla of Boston, Pittsburgh's Roberto Clemente, Minnesota's Tony Oliva, Cookie Rojas of the Phillies, me, Minnesota's Zoilo Versalles, Vic Davalillo of the Indians, and Leo Cardenas of the Reds. *Herb Scharfman/Sports Illustrated/Getty Images*

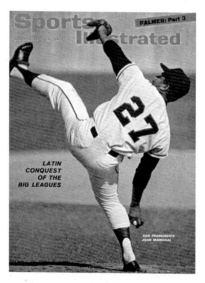

By 1965, Latin players in the majors were getting national attention. This issue of *Sports Illustrated* from August 1965 featured me on the cover for an article entitled "The Latins Storm *Las Grandes Ligas*." *Neil Leifer, SI Cover/ Sports Illustrated/Getty Images*

Here I give Willie Mays a hug after he ended my 16-inning marathon with Warren Spahn of the Braves on July 3, 1963. Willie's home run ended the 1–0 game after more than four hours. *AP Images*

Winning my 200th game was a highlight of my major league career. *Sal Veder/AP Images*

When I went home during the winters between major league seasons, I often helped out at a youth baseball clinic at the local college, Universidad Autonoma de Santo Domingo, to give the young players some tips. *Marichal collection*

I always tried to sign autographs and spend time with the fans, especially the young ones, to show my appreciation for their coming out to support me and the team. This is at Candlestick Park in 1966. *Marichal collection*

Getting inducted into the Baseball Hall of Fame and getting a plaque alongside all those incredible players was one of the greatest thrills of my life. *Marichal collection*

I was honored to be named to the Major League Baseball Latino Legends team in 2005. Among the other honorees in attendance for the celebration at that year's World Series in Houston were (from left next to me) Fernando Valenzuela, Pedro Martinez, Ivan Rodriguez, Rod Carew, Alex Rodriguez, Edgar Martinez, and Roberto Clemente, represented by his sons Luis and Roberto Jr. *Eric Gay/AP Images*

Although I'm not as limber as I used to be, here I try to
re-create my pitching style during the dedication of my statue
outside San Francisco's AT&T Park in 2005—a very proud
moment for me. *Brad Mangin/Sports Illustrated/Getty Images*

It's always great to get together with my former teammates. On Opening Day of the 2007 season, I was joined by Gaylord Perry and Willie McCovey, among others, in a ceremony honoring former Giants all-stars and Hall of Famers. *Jed Jacobsohn/ Getty Images*

My charity golf tournaments in the Dominican draw big stars from the United States. Mariano Duncan (left) and Barry Bonds (right) played in the 2007 event. *Jorge Cruz/AP Images*

What a beautiful family I have! Standing behind me and Alma are our six children: Rosie, Elsie, Charlene, Juan Antonio, Ursula, and Yvette. *Marichal collection*

Roger Guenveur Smith, who portrayed both Johnny and me in *Juan and John*, is a very good actor. He did a wonderful job. I went to New York and saw the play there, and President Fernandez and first lady Doña Margarita of the Dominican were with me. They invited him to bring the play to the Dominican, which he did. It showed in front of a crowd of 400, and Dominican ballplayers Ubaldo Jimenez and Miguel Batista were in the audience.

I love the play. I like the way it worked. It made me cry.

It started with a kid whose idol was Johnny Roseboro, and after he heard what I did with the bat he burned my baseball card. That man really did that. In the play he saved that card, and at the end he had it and the message was forgiveness. It's a very beautiful story. It was very well done, and my family and the actor have become close.

In the play I said I wished Johnny Roseboro had been my catcher. After I saw the play, Bruce Weber from the *New York Times* asked me if I had really said that. I did.

CHAPTER 10

Back to Normal, Back to Dominance

Juan Marichal had established himself as one of the best pitchers in baseball with his spectacular 25-win season in 1963. Proving he wasn't a one-hit wonder, he followed that with a 21–8 record in 1964. The Giants ace was extremely tough to score on during those two seasons, compiling ERAs of 2.41 and 2.48.

As could be expected, Marichal earned as much attention for the Johnny Roseboro incident as he did for his accomplishments on the mound in 1965. Despite the suspension, he won 22 games and pitched a league- and career-best 10 shutouts. At 2.13, his earned run average in 1965 was one of the lowest of his career.

The Roseboro incident was haunting, but after the winter break and renewing himself in the Dominican, Marichal seemed back to his normal self in 1966 and had another extraordinary year on the mound. His record was 25–6. He pitched 307⅓ innings and struck out 240 batters. His winning percentage of .806 was the finest in the game.

Marichal prided himself on being ready to pitch every fourth day. He consistently took the ball a full complement of games during the 154-game (and then 162-game) season, and he hated to give up the ball once he started. During his prime, he completed as many games as any National League starter.

Along with Sandy Koufax, Marichal was the most consistently great hurler during the 1960s. By the time it was over, Marichal's 191 victories made him the winningest pitcher of the decade. Koufax and Marichal are the only two pitchers who have won 25 or more games in a season two or more times since World War II.

Over time, Marichal's steady all-star-level performance gained him appreciation from baseball fans and experts. On June 10, 1966, Marichal was featured on the cover of Time *magazine. The editors called him "The Dandy Dominican," a description Marichal was never fond of. He also didn't especially care for the more common "Dominican Dandy."*

Even with Marichal's dazzling work on the mound, and the other tremendous players on the Giants roster, those years proved ultimately frustrating, as San Francisco was unable to regain pennant-winning form. The first half of the 1960s was a very competitive time in the National League, with the pennant changing hands every year. Unlike in the American League, where the Yankees controlled the top of the standings for years on end, the senior circuit had a different "top dog" with each new season.

The Pittsburgh Pirates took the pennant in 1960. The Cincinnati Reds won it in 1961. The Giants seized the moment in 1962. The Dodgers won in 1963 and the Cardinals in 1964. That made five different World Series representatives in five years before the Dodgers and Cardinals ruled the rest of the decade, with back-to-back pennants by Los Angeles in 1965 and 1966 and by St. Louis in 1967 and 1968.

There were only eight teams in the league until 1962, when the New York Mets and the Houston Colt .45s (later the Astros) joined as expansion franchises to make it 10. Every team had great players, and the Giants had their share. Marichal was fortunate to have a lineup hitting for him that was loaded with sluggers, hitters who knew their roles, and future Hall of Famers.

But he also pitched regularly against some of the greatest hitters of all time, including Hank Aaron and Eddie Mathews of the Braves, Roberto Clemente of the Pirates, and Frank Robinson of the Reds. They all had able supporting casts that made it difficult to cruise through the lineup. Although the Chicago Cubs finished near the bottom of the standings throughout the early 1960s, their order was anchored by dangerous hitters such as Ernie Banks, Billy Williams, and Ron Santo—no easy outs there.

Opposing players knew better than anyone how good Marichal was. In the four years ending with 1965, when Sandy Koufax was being called the best pitcher of his generation, Marichal won 86 games and Koufax won 84.

Joe Morgan, the Hall of Fame second baseman who was then with Houston and later spent a generation visiting living rooms as a baseball broadcaster, said both were hard to hit. "When you get a hit off of either one," Morgan once said, "the umpire should stop the game and present you with the ball."

Marichal's manager, Herman Franks, summed up his ace's effectiveness with a fact that knowledgeable observers recognized for years. "No man has the assortment of pitches Juan has," Franks said.

WILLIE MAYS WAS THE GREATEST PLAYER EVER. THE WAY HE PLAYED THE GAME, WITH BOTH HIS HEART AND HIS HEAD, IS one thing that made him great. He had that special instinct in the outfield where, at the sound of the ball on the bat, he knew right away where to go. He used to run and even turn his back and get to the ball so it landed right in his glove in front of him, belt high. He had that basket catch. To do that you have to have instinct, and Willie was almost perfect with that.

He could hit. He could run. He could throw. And he didn't need any coaching when he was running the bases. He knew how far he could go when somebody hit the ball to left field. He knew if he could go to second or go to third when someone hit it to right field. He played the game so well, and he knew how to play every opponent. That was his greatest strength. Willie made my career easy. When I was pitching, Willie and the catcher and I held a three-man meeting. He told us how to pitch each individual. He knew where he was going to play them.

Off the field and in the locker room Willie was shy, very shy. But he was very generous, especially to the guys who weren't making much money. Because he was Willie Mays, lots of people gave him stuff for free. They invited him places. They gave him free clothing. Willie got everything for free. In the clubhouse if someone needed gloves or shoes, they would go to Willie. In those days, a regular player might only get two gloves or two pairs of shoes for the season. Willie got whatever he wanted. A lot of people wanted to use his bats. Whoever wanted a bat got one. He was the type of guy who would take the whole team to a men's clothing store, and everyone would leave with at least one suit. The stores gave Willie anything he wanted.

He could have had a free meal anywhere he wanted to go, but Willie very seldom went to a restaurant. When we were on the road, he would rather have hotel room service instead of eating out, because everyone would want to see him and talk to him. When we went out with Willie, people got wild. They wanted a picture with Willie. They wanted to get close to Willie. And Willie was shy about that.

Willie was more fun in the locker room, though. He had fun with everybody. He made some jokes, but he really liked to listen to jokes. He laughed so hard at other guys' jokes. Pitchers Ray Sadecki and Mike McCormick were always joking, and they made him roar. They told jokes and played tricks. They made everyone in the clubhouse laugh.

They did crazy things, Ray and Mike. They had a routine where they would come in and pretend to be a dead chicken. They also would bring a little box and sit down next to you and you could hear a telephone ring inside the box. They opened the box and handed you the telephone and said it was for you. They bought powder that stinks something awful. They would get in the elevator when they knew there would be other people in it and they would drop the powder and get out. People would get into the elevator and smell something terrible. It got into your eyes and you started sneezing.

Those guys, let me tell you, they were pretty funny. They liked practical jokes. I did some of the same kind of things, the practical jokes, the pranks. I hit players with towels when they were coming out of the shower. I stole car keys and hid them. Sometimes I set off firecrackers. You should have seen the way Willie McCovey jumped up in the air. It was all in good fun for us. Willie Mays didn't play too many jokes, but he liked to laugh at all the others.

Orlando focused more on the music. He was the clubhouse music man. He always had a record player with him wherever he went, and he would bring a box of records when we traveled. It was mostly jazz. He always made a rookie carry the box of records.

Matty Alou was Orlando's roommate for a while and he used to tell us he couldn't get enough sleep because Orlando would get up in the middle of the night, any time of the night, and play music. Matty said he actually enjoyed the music, but when the music stopped Orlando would start clapping.

Willie McCovey is a great man. They called him "Stretch" because he was tall and he stretched out to catch throws at first base. Everybody likes Stretch. He always loved to laugh. In 1959, when he was a rookie with the Giants, he came to the Dominican Republic and played with Escogido. I met him there before we were on the Giants together. We became good friends. Willie Mac—I call him Willie Mac—was a friend of everybody. He was such a powerful man, too. He hit home runs that were so high you thought they were never going to come down. When he retired in 1980 with 521 career home runs, only seven people in baseball history had hit more home runs than Stretch.

We had a very good lineup with Willie Mays, Orlando, Willie Mac, Felipe Alou, and Jim Davenport. Jim had one of the best gloves at third base. He had strong hands and knew how to play the game. He and his wife were really close friends with Alma and me. He loved to play golf, and was quite good at that, too.

I started to play golf because of Jim. He played all the time. Every afternoon after practice he and Jack Hiatt and a couple of other guys went to play golf. At the time I didn't know how to play, so I rented a golf cart to follow them and watch and just hang out with them.

After watching them—they were good golfers—I became interested in learning how to play. That's how I started to play golf. Now I have my own golf tournament every January in the Dominican to raise money for charity.

We had one other big hitter who was underrated compared to those other guys. Jim Ray Hart. He was another guy with a lot of power. Everybody laughed with Jim Ray Hart. He didn't say much, but he had this one saying. Whenever he talked about something he said, "Wait in line." That was his line. Very seldom would you hear him say something, but then, all of a sudden, he would say that. He was quiet, but what a hitter. He had no fear. It didn't matter who was pitching. He hit with so much power. When he was a rookie in 1964, he hit 31 home runs—the same as Orlando and more than Willie Mac that year.

Jack Sanford was a great pitcher at his best. In 1962, he won 24 games. He had good control and a good slider, and he knew how to pitch. He was somebody you wanted to watch and learn from. He was that kind of pitcher.

We had Billy Pierce for only a couple years after he came over from the White Sox, but he was on the 1962 World Series team. What a human being. Such a nice guy. Every time he went to the mound, you knew he meant business. In 1962 he helped us win the pennant. He won 16 games for us that year. Great personality and a good friend; a very smart man.

Stu Miller was the best relief pitcher at the time, before there were closers and relief specialists. That guy had a change-up I couldn't believe. Nobody could hit his change-up. You knew it was coming, but you couldn't hit it because he was so far ahead of you.

I remember Stu Miller against Frank Howard when he was with the Dodgers. Stu was about 5-foot-10 and Frank Howard was about 6-foot-7. He looked like a giant in the batter's box. I remember a change-up he threw to Frank. Somebody took a picture of it, and you could see Frank Howard's bat already over the plate and the ball was still five feet from the plate. It hadn't gotten to the plate yet and he had already swung. Unbelievable. Nobody threw a change-up like Stu Miller. I think the secret was in his hand motion. He moved his hand so hard that the hitter started swinging before the ball got there.

You know how baseball announcers on radio and TV always talk about "the book" on a hitter? When I got to the majors, I started keeping a little black book of my own that I wrote in whenever I pitched or whenever I saw guys play.

I actually had two books. They were pretty big. I kept one at home and one in the clubhouse. Every time I faced a team, I wrote something down so the next time I could look at it and have some knowledge about them. I always put the box score in there. If I was watching a hitter against another pitcher and he got him out four times right away, I knew what to throw. I figured out how to get that man out. I tried to do the same thing as he did. Sometimes it worked.

You had to study. There were too many good hitters on every team. Today in baseball you see a lot of good hitters, but some of them are on the team because there are more players. When there were only eight teams in each league, there were so many good hitters and so many good pitchers. There was no room to relax.

Today there are 30 teams, and they need so many pitchers in the bullpen. Some are not ready for the major leagues. That's why I think the hitters have an advantage.

When it was my turn to start a game against a certain team, the first thing I did was go to the notebook to read my notes and remind myself how I should pitch certain hitters in certain situations. That book had everything in it, and I knew in some situations I might have to try something new to get a guy out. You always have to try new things. Even if the guy is a good hitter, you have to keep trying.

If the other team had a new player and I didn't have him in the book, I wanted information on that player—where he came from, where he played, what type of hitter he was, what type of ball he liked to hit. I was looking for any type of edge I could have when I faced a hitter for the first time. I think pitchers have always been interested in knowing something about hitters.

Whenever I was pitching, I would keep a strict routine, a schedule that I followed. Remember the discipline I learned in the Air Force.

Part of my preparation when I was due to pitch was looking in my book the night before and then going to bed early. My routine included thinking about the game and running through the lineup I would face the next day. I went to bed at eight or nine o'clock and I didn't have any trouble falling asleep. I got up at 8 or 8:30 in the morning.

Once you get up in the morning on the day you pitch, the only thing you are thinking about is baseball. The most important thing for me was making sure I stuck to the routine, especially with food, because I didn't want to feel heavy when I went to the mound.

In the Dominican, for breakfast, we would have two eggs with plantain, maybe boiled. It was like a mashed potato, but made from plantain. You can mash them and make them really soft. I was able to get that in San Francisco because there was a store nearby called Luka Supermarket. We went there all the time to buy products like we had at home. I added a little oil, onions, and salt to my eggs and plantain, and maybe had some coffee with milk in it.

If I was going to pitch a night game I ate no later than four o'clock. My dinner was steak with a baked potato, a little bit of vegetable, maybe green beans. That was the plan I followed.

Two days before I was scheduled to pitch I trimmed my fingernails. I didn't want any blisters on my fingers. If you don't take care of your fingernails, one can break and you start bleeding. Then you have to stop pitching. If the blood got on the ball the umpire was going to find out what was happening, and you could be out of the game because of that. That's why it was important to trim the fingernails neatly. I was always very careful with my fingernails and my food. You want to feel good and relaxed and free to do your work.

For a day game that started at one o'clock at Candlestick Park, I got there between 9:30 and 10 in the morning. When other guys got to the clubhouse, sometimes I played cards with them. That was to keep my mind occupied once I was ready. You don't want to overthink it. I had already thought about the team, and I wanted to keep my mind clear for a little while. After I played cards I went to the training room to get a massage. I thought that was very important. The trainer used to put baby oil on my body, and if it was cold I used a heat treatment on top of that.

Before batting practice I met with the catcher and we went over the other team's hitters. Sometimes it was very quick because we knew who they were, especially if we had played against them recently.

Then I went outside for batting practice and bunting practice. I concentrated on the hit-and-run because I might be asked to move a runner ahead. That would be very important if the leadoff hitter was coming up after me and the runner was in good position. I hate to see a pitcher today who is not able to move a runner forward. That player doesn't belong in the major leagues. Sometimes they're not practicing or sometimes they just don't want to do it.

After batting practice, I had some time back in the locker room to get ready, and then it was game time. I was so happy to be on the mound. I couldn't wait to get there; I ran from the bench to the mound. Nobody else was doing that until I came to the major leagues. You know why I started to do that? When the inning is over and you get to the mound, you don't get your regular catcher if he is changing his gear. I had another person to catch me. By running out to the mound the umpire was not at home plate. You're entitled to throw so many warm-up pitches, but I could throw a few more because he wasn't paying attention. That was one reason I ran to the mound. Plus, I was just happy to be out there.

In the baseball movie *For the Love of the Game*, Kevin Costner is a pitcher and he talks to himself a lot on the mound. Great movie. I talked to myself on the mound sometimes, too. If the catcher gave a sign and I wasn't able to throw the ball where he wanted it, I would talk to myself. I'd say, "Come on, Juan. You're better than that. You've got better control than that." I told Tom Haller and Ed Bailey any time they wanted a pitch in a certain place and I didn't throw it where they wanted it, to fire the ball back to me. "Tell me you're not happy with that," I said. They used to do it.

We had those two catchers for a long time and I was comfortable with both of them. I never had control problems. It didn't matter who was behind the plate. Bailey told a lot of jokes, but Haller didn't have too many. He was happy to hear them in the clubhouse, though. Ed made you laugh to break the tension, and Tom was a different type.

I had five pitches, so the catchers had a lot of signs. I used to throw a curve on one and a fastball on two, the opposite of other pitchers. I did it because in those days coaches tried to steal signs more than they do today. If I wanted to throw a screwball, No. 5, I had to say no again and again until we got to the screwball. I liked to pitch quickly, so to save time I invented signs where I touched my chest and leg with my glove. That was our secret sign.

The catcher and pitcher both call the game. We used to work really well together, me and my catchers. The catcher would call the pitch, but I was entitled to switch it. Not every day are your pitches equally effective. Some days one of your pitches might not be working. So you want to stay away from that one.

Overall, you can tell if the ball is moving well and if you have better control on the fastball or slider, or better control on the screwball. There was always some time during the season when my screwball wasn't working because I couldn't get the right grip. I might go four or five innings without using the screwball, and after five innings I would try it again. If it felt good and it was working, I threw more screwballs. I might change during the game.

Which pitches I threw also depended on the hitters. On a given day you might stay away from one type of pitch because the hitter specializes in hitting it.

You can confuse hitters if they face you a couple of times in a game and you do not throw one certain pitch, and then they come to the plate a third time and you start throwing that pitch. That's the science of pitching. Pitching is about more than just throwing a fastball past a hitter. A lot of people don't understand that. Some pitchers these days have only two pitches. Some of the relievers really just throw one. Mariano Rivera has a cut fastball and a fastball, and he is so great. You know why? Control. Almost all the time he can throw the ball where he wants to, and he knows how to pitch.

If you have good control, you throw the ball at least seven times in ten to where the catcher wants it to be thrown. If you miss three times, that's okay. When the catcher is waiting for the ball and the pitch is not a strike, sometimes he can move the glove quickly from here to there and confuse the umpire.

Umpires sometimes go by the movement of the catcher. The ball could be in the strike zone, but if the catcher has the glove over here and he has to move it, the umpire might call a ball. If you miss inside or outside, but the glove doesn't come from inside to outside, that's bad.

I watch a lot of games on TV and I know the umpires miss so many pitches. They know the pitcher throwing the ball. They know what kind of pitcher he is. The call should be made based not on where the ball ends up but where it crosses the plate. Sometimes the ball crosses the plate and moves inside or outside, but when it crossed the plate it already hit the strike zone. That should be a strike. Sometimes a ball might be right in the middle of the plate but end up in the dirt, and is called a ball.

I knew the umpires, too. There were some calls I knew I wasn't going to get depending on the umpire. I used to have a move to first base when a runner was on and it was an illegal move. I did it on purpose many times, and only one umpire called a balk on me. That was Doug Harvey, and he got inducted into the Hall of Fame in 2010. He was the best umpire I ever pitched to. When he was an umpire on the bases, I never made that pickoff move because I knew he would call a balk. I would do it when he was behind home plate, because the plate umpire doesn't call a balk on that kind of move, only the base umpire.

When I first came up to the majors and when I did most of my playing, there was no free agency. That meant that players stayed with their teams more than they do now. You didn't have a chance to play out your option to get a new contract from another team if your team wanted to keep you.

A lot of guys stayed with their teams for years and years, and they were identified with those teams. I knew if we were playing the Pirates we were going to see Roberto Clemente. I knew if we were playing the Braves we were going to see Hank Aaron. Those guys weren't going anywhere. The only way you really got to know them was at the All-Star Game if you were all representing the National League—and guys like Clemente and Aaron were on the team every year back then. We talked a lot during the break, but we went our own ways again and faced each other on the field when it was over. Maybe we saw each other in the winter at a dinner or a banquet if we were invited to the same one. Mostly they hit against me and I pitched against them.

Sometimes I was just like another fan, especially after I retired. I would hear the name of a certain player and liked the sound of it. Catfish Hunter with the A's and Yankees was one of those guys. I loved to listen to that name. He came to my golf tournament and that's how we got to know each other. Duke Snider of the Dodgers, who played one year with the Giants. They called him the "Duke of Destruction." I liked to hear that name. He came to my golf classic. Duke Snider was a very good bad-ball hitter.

Another name that I loved to hear when I was a kid was Sal Maglie, the pitcher. They called him "The Barber." He liked to pitch hitters tight and was good at giving them a close shave. Boy, I used to love to hear those names. I didn't know them, but they were my idols. I always watched the *Game of the Week*, and after I came to the major leagues I asked about those guys and read about them.

Roberto Clemente became a friend. We got together when the Latin players mixed.

Frank Robinson of the Reds was underrated. He was such a great, great hitter. He used to stand close to the plate and get hit by a lot of pitches. He got hit, but he never charged the mound. He walked to first base, but whoever covered second base when he was coming had to watch out. I guess that's how he got revenge for getting hit by a pitch. He was going fast and whoever caught that ball at second had to be careful. Robinson was tough.

I got to know Frank Robinson through the All-Star Game. He was very intense and quiet. He might joke around a little bit, but a lot of times you thought he was mad or something. Baseball players had a lot of respect for him. Let me say this about Frank Robinson: That guy won the Triple Crown in both leagues, first with the Reds and then with the Baltimore Orioles. To do that, you have to be awesome, and he was.

Vada Pinson, who also played for Cincinnati for many years, was even more underrated than Frank Robinson. Pinson was a good, good ballplayer. He ran so fast I couldn't believe it. He was a great hitter, too, and played well in the outfield.

Hank Aaron, they called him "The Hammer." He was so natural the way he swung the bat. He didn't hit the ball 500 feet, but he hit it long enough to go over the wall. A great all-around player. That man played year after year and he never seemed to get hurt. He was very consistent at a very high level. I have a lot of respect for him. Once in a while he hit a home run off of me and beat me in a ballgame, but I think if you look at the numbers I might have been a little bit ahead of him.

Ernie Banks, "Mr. Cub," is a great human being. He is a very happy man, I think. He loves the game. He always said, "It's a lovely day for baseball. Let's play two." You could tell on the field that Ernie Banks had a positive attitude. He also came to my golf tournament in the Dominican.

Billy Williams was also with the Cubs and a very tough hitter to get out back then. "Sweet Swinging Billy Williams," they called him. Every time he came up to the plate he was dragging his bat like there was something wrong with him, like he didn't have any energy and couldn't even lift the bat. Then, on the first pitch, that man hit the ball a long distance. He used a 31-ounce bat. Very light. I used to get a bat from him. I liked his bat. He was such a good hitter. I think he was a little bit in the shadow of Ernie Banks, but the guy hit hundreds of home runs and is now in the Hall of Fame. Billy Williams was a great hitter, but according to my book I got him out very, very often.

I got to know Johnny Bench because he caught me a few times in the All-Star Game. I loved to watch him behind home plate. He was like a wall back there. It was impossible for me to throw the ball past him, he was such a good fielder. He would give pitchers confidence. It made it easier for them to pitch. I wish I could have thrown to him more in my day.

I loved to watch Carl Yastrzemski hit. He had that batting stance where he held the bat so high up in the air. I was his teammate when I played one year with Boston, and we became good friends then. There were a lot of good guys on the Red Sox: Carlton Fisk, Luis Tiant, Diego Segui.

Some guys, though, if you played your whole career in the National League and they played theirs in the American League, you might never get to meet. Harmon Killebrew was one of those guys. I might never have met him, but I pitched against him in the 1965 All-Star Game in Minnesota. I hit it off with him. We became close friends, too. But that was mostly later through the Hall of Fame, going back for visits each summer. I read so much about Harmon Killebrew and his many home runs that I thought I knew him. He was the king of home runs in the American League. He hit 573 in his career. He hit 40 eight times, and that was when nobody used steroids. That's why they called him "Killer."

We did treat the All-Star Game more seriously than the players do now, I think. In those days, before the game, the president of the National League would come into the clubhouse and give us one of those pep talks about how we had to win and beat the American League. We had to do this. It was very important to us. That was pride. Winning the All-Star Game was supposed to show that you were superior. I don't know if it did, but at the time we beat them so many times. During my 14 years with the Giants, the National League beat the American League 14 times, and they won only two times. [From 1959 to 1962, there were two All-Star Games each season.]

Some people said the reason we won all the time is because the National League was more integrated than the American League. The Giants, Pirates, and Dodgers had more black and Latin players, and we had a lot of good ones from other teams like Ernie Banks, Hank Aaron, and Frank Robinson. Maybe that was it. We never talked about it. There were a lot of good black and Latin players then.

Willie Stargell of the Pirates was a good human being and a good hitter. I used to get Willie Stargell out easily. I could read his mind. I knew what he was looking for. He wanted a pitch from the middle of the plate out. I never threw those pitches to him. I threw fastballs inside where he couldn't get them. Once he saw the ball inside, he was looking for that pitch and then I went with a screwball. I confused him many times. He was fun to be around. He was loose, a very different type of guy than Bob Gibson of the Cardinals, who was very intense.

The St. Louis Cardinals were very good in the 1960s, but I didn't feel like I was facing a team, I felt like I was facing Bob Gibson. Every time he was on the mound you knew he wanted to win. He played fiercely. He was like Don Drysdale. He didn't care about coming close to hitting the batters with his fastball. They called Gibson "The Head Hunter" and he loved to be called that. He loved that name. He wasn't trying to hurt the batters, but he wanted to make them nervous. It was okay with him if they thought of him like that. That was to his advantage.

Bob Gibson was all business. He didn't mess around. He took the game so seriously. He joined the Cardinals in 1959, the year before I came up to the Giants. The first time I faced St. Louis in my career was in 1960 and I pitched against Gibson. I pitched a complete game and we won.

The Cardinals were a great team then. They won three pennants in the 1960s. St. Louis also helped us win the pennant in 1962. We were fighting the Dodgers for first place. In the last game the Cardinals played in San Francisco that year, Stan Musial went 5-for-5 and they beat us. But then they went to Los Angeles and beat the Dodgers three times, and that's how we caught the Dodgers in the standings.

I only pitched against Musial at the very end of his career. "Stan the Man," they called him. I got him out the first time I faced him, in 1960.

The Cardinals were a very balanced team. Ken Boyer was the third baseman. Bill White was the first baseman. Lou Brock came over from the Cubs in the outfield. What a player. The guy stole so many bases. He held the record for a while with 938. He had a little bit of power, but he was a good hitter. Tim McCarver, now well known as a broadcaster, was the catcher.

One of their guys I knew very well was Julian Javier, whose son Stan also played in the majors. Julian was a good friend of mine. He played second base and he was underrated, too. He was an awesome fielder, and you should have seen him run from second base to home plate. He was the best.

I liked Pete Rose. He hustled all the time, the way you're supposed to play the game. He was with the "Big Red Machine" in Cincinnati, and what a player. People always ask him, "Who was the best pitcher you faced?" and he said "Juan Marichal." People ask me "Who was the best hitter you faced?" and I say, "Pete Rose." I mean it. He was the best hitter in baseball. He got 4,256 hits.

Too bad Pete Rose is not in the Hall of Fame. I think he should be. Oh yes, he should be. He has paid enough of a penalty. He was wrong to gamble on baseball. It is too bad he was so stubborn. I talked to Pete many times and he is really very sorry. He did say he was sorry, but too late. I know he should be in there. I like Pete very much. He played so hard.

He was disciplined at the plate. He would swing at nothing but good pitches. He figured out when the slider was coming and he never went for that pitch. He had so much determination. I got to know Pete well. He was the type who wore his emotions on his sleeve. The thing about him was his hustle. Even with a walk, he ran to first base like he was going for a double. I like that type of player.

I say that Pete Rose was the best hitter I faced, but the hardest hitter for me to get out was a guy that not too many people would guess. It works that way sometimes, that the guy who is not the best can hit you the best. Tony Gonzalez was like that for me, the outfielder who played mostly for the Phillies. His lifetime average was .286, but I couldn't get him out. He hit the ball all over the field. First a ball through the middle, then sometimes a bullet to the outfield. He swung hard, but he wasn't wild.

Eddie Mathews, the third baseman for the Braves who hit more than 500 home runs, hit very well against me. Orlando likes to tell a story about me pitching against Mathews. One time with the game on the line, Mathews came to the plate and Orlando came over to the mound and said, "Juan, be careful with this guy, he kills the fastball." I told Juan I needed a strikeout and to get a strikeout I had to throw a fastball. So I threw Mathews three fastballs and I struck him out. Orlando couldn't believe it.

One thing I could never figure out is why, when they put in the designated hitter rule, it was only in the American League. It should have been in both leagues. Very strange. Major League Baseball should be played with the same rules.

There are always times that come up when you have to send a message to the other team and throw an inside fastball. When we were playing, we didn't throw at their best hitter. We threw at the other pitcher most of the time. We waited until the pitcher got in the batter's box. We would throw at him and they would throw at me and that stopped the whole thing right there. With the designated hitter, you can't do that because the pitcher never comes up.

I had these big matchups with Sandy Koufax and Don Drysdale of the Dodgers, Bob Gibson and Warren Spahn, but there were other guys who were really tough. Lew Burdette with the Braves was one of them, and Jim Maloney with the Reds used to throw so hard.

When people ask me how fast I threw, I tell them that I didn't really know because they didn't have the radar guns on me. I knew that when I really needed to strike somebody out with a fastball, I did it. Maybe I could throw 95 or 96 mph when I had to do it. Maybe because I used five different pitches my velocity didn't show the speed. I got more of that velocity when I threw a fastball or a slider. But I also threw the breaking ball, the sidearm change-up, and those off-speed pitches.

CHAPTER 11

Disappointments and Triumphs

*W*hen Juan Marichal broke in with the San Francisco Giants in 1960, Felipe Alou, one of his best friends from childhood, was with the team. Eventually, in 1964, Alou was traded. The Latin players, who revered his influence and looked up to him as a leader, resented it.

At least as shocking for Marichal was the departure of his pal Orlando Cepeda in a trade to the St. Louis Cardinals, a swap that fizzled for the Giants. St. Louis got a future Hall of Famer and San Francisco got a pitcher, Ray Sadecki, who was a good guy in the locker room but who made no serious impact for them on the mound.

As great as the two hitters were, the Giants had struggled for years about how best to use Cepeda and Willie

McCovey in the lineup together. They were terrific sluggers, but both were natural first basemen. With no designated hitter, playing the one not assigned to first base that day was a constant dilemma. The compromise was to put either Cepeda or McCovey in the outfield. It was neither man's best position, and they were not superb fielders out on the grass.

The Giants decided to "solve" the problem once and for all by sending Cepeda to St. Louis on May 8, 1966, for Sadecki. Cepeda helped lead the Cardinals to the World Series in 1967, and he won the National League Most Valuable Player Award that year. Sadecki went 3–7 with San Francisco in 1966. Although he did go 12–6 in 1967, the trade—fairly or not—has been labeled one of the worst of all time.

Marichal missed his old friend and lamented Cepeda's departure as much as he had Alou's. These were the kinds of developments that came with the territory in baseball, however. He was mature enough to recognize that.

After his 25-win campaign in 1966, Marichal had a difficult season in 1967, finishing just 14–10 despite again posting an exceptional earned run average of 2.76. Injuries limited him to 26 starts and played a role in that off-year. However, Marichal bounced back phenomenally in 1968. He recorded his career high for wins with 26, his career high in complete games with 30, and his career high of 325⅔ innings pitched. All three marks led the National League. His sparkling earned run average of 2.43 ranked in the top 10 among National Leaguers during the famous "Year of the Pitcher"—when Bob Gibson led the majors with an incredible mark of 1.12.

As the years passed, the challenge of staying healthy was Marichal's greatest frustration. His biggest obstacle was keeping his body finely tuned when fluke things occurred. Marichal did not suffer from a sore arm, despite pitching so many innings. But he had other injuries that impeded him. Sometimes they were small ones, sometimes large ones. At times, cynical sportswriters questioned how seriously hurt he was, and Marichal bristled at any suggestion that he might be a malingerer. Similarly, if any coach or manager didn't trust his own analysis of his health, such lack of faith disturbed him.

Marichal could point to his own large volume of innings pitched every year and how he fought to stay in contests to pitch complete games as evidence of his desire to be out on the mound. But no one has a perfect career, and no one can stay 100 percent healthy for every step of a 16-year journey. Things happen.

Through the various struggles to stay healthy, one of Marichal's greatest moments during the latter part of his career was his 200th win in 1970. After the victory, a grinning Marichal posed for a picture holding up a game ball with the number 200 written on it. The win was his sixth in a row at the time, and it followed an earlier stretch when he had been weakened by illness. The milestone made Marichal reflect again about how far he had come since his youth in the Dominican.

Now, as his career entered its latter half, new disappointments and experiences emerged.

When the Giants traded Orlando to St. Louis I was very upset. We all were. We were playing the Cardinals, and at the end of the series, they traded him. He got the word after the last game and went across the field to their dugout. Just like that.

I put my arm around Orlando's shoulder and said, "No way this can be true. They aren't trading you." But it was. When we got to the clubhouse there was a press conference to acknowledge the trade. We were both crying.

The next time we played the Cardinals, Orlando was starting for them. We had been teammates and now we were opponents. My turn in the pitching rotation came up while we were playing St. Louis, and I spent the day wondering what I was going to throw to him because he knew everything I did.

I invited him out to eat first and then we went to our different clubhouses before the game. The first time he came to the plate, the first pitch, I knocked him down. I threw it right inside on him. You should have seen the look in his eye. I couldn't stop laughing. I had to turn around and face center field. We never forgot that. Every time we get together he has to say something about it. He always brings that up. I tell him that when I released the ball, I yelled, "Watch out!" That was funny. He went into the dirt.

He always says, "Remember the next pitch?" I say, "Yeah, you hit a ground ball for an out." He says, "I hit it out of the stadium." [In truth, Cepeda grounded out in the first at bat but did homer off Marichal later in the game.]

After that, he did hit me pretty well. He got two home runs off of me during his career. He likes to say it was three, but it was two. One of those was much later when he was in Atlanta, playing with the Braves. I was winning 5–0 in the ninth inning. When he came to the plate I began joking with him. I said, "I'll let you hit the ball because I feel sorry for you." I threw a fastball and he hit that ball so far to right field, it was unbelievable. He hit it so far I couldn't believe it. So I won 5–1 and I always tell him, "I let you hit that one. I felt sorry for you." He was a great hitter. He had power to all fields.

I had to pitch against Felipe, too, and he got me pretty good. [Felipe hit .305 with three home runs in 59 at bats against Marichal. The three Alou brothers batted a combined .333 against him in 144 at bats.]

After I won 26 games to lead the league in 1968, I won 21 games the next year. That was the sixth time I won more than 20 games in the big leagues. My earned run average that year was 2.10. That led the majors and was the best of my career.

Most of those years, except for 1967, I was healthy all season long, but sometimes I had small problems and other times different parts of my body gave me trouble. During my career I never had a big sore arm like those guys who have Tommy John surgery or need major repairs on their throwing arms. But I had my share of other injuries that sometimes slowed me down.

My back was a problem off and on for years. That is a tough injury, because most of the time you can't tell what is really going on with it. You can't point to the spot and see a broken bone or a pulled muscle, and sometimes even the trainer can't tell you what is going on. The Giants kept sending me to doctors to find out what was wrong with my back. One moment my back hurt and another it was fine. I put up with it until 1972, when the doctors told me I had to have surgery on my back.

I got hit by a line drive that Duke Snider hit and I hurt my Achilles tendon. It could have been worse, and it healed fine. I also had a broken right foot in 1962. It hurt, but they could never see what was wrong and some people didn't believe that there was something wrong. Four years later they found it. I was pitching against Cincinnati and Tommy Helms hit me with a line drive. I finished the game, but afterward they took me to a hospital and that's when they found the old fracture.

One time we were on the road in Pittsburgh and I woke up in the hotel in the morning and the right side of my face was swollen. So I went to see the trainer and showed him. He looked at it and said, "Juan, let's wait until tomorrow before I take you to the doctor." So the next day I got up and both sides of my face were swollen.

The doctor told me I had the mumps—the illness that kids get. The doctor said I had the mumps, but the trainer disagreed. I was scheduled to pitch that night and I did. I won the game. Four days later, in Milwaukee, I had to pitch against the Braves. I won again.

The team was still on a road trip, but they sent me back to San Francisco because I was still sick. The doctor there examined me and said, sure enough, I had the mumps. He was very mad at the team for having me pitch those two games. He said, "How can they do that? You could have infected the whole team. They could have ruined your whole career." He said that the mumps not only could have made my teammates sick, they could have spread to my testicles and I might not have been able to have children. None of that happened, thank God. I did pitch two games with the mumps.

Besides that illness, I had one injury that did not come from baseball. I was with Manny Mota one time and, as we were getting out of a car, he slammed the door on my pitching hand. Boy, did that hurt. I was so mad. It was after a game in San Francisco, a day game, and we were going out to eat.

I couldn't play for a while. We went on a road trip to New York to play the Mets, and we kept putting relief pitchers in and the Mets kept hitting them. Herman Franks came up to me and said, "Do you want to throw an inning?" I said, "I think I can."

I liked working with Herman as my manager. He was a very different type from Alvin Dark. Herman believed in me, and when there was something he wanted to say he always did it face to face.

That was one of the few times in my whole career that I pitched in relief. He got me in the game and we started hitting and won the game. I got the win in relief. I usually remember everything, but that is the only game I remember pitching in relief, even though there were others. [Juan Marichal started all but 14 of the 471 games in which he pitched.]

One time I had a reaction to penicillin. When we traveled to Japan for an exhibition tour in 1970, it was cold and I got a throat infection. We were flying back to the United States, and after we landed in San Francisco we went on to Palm Springs for a series of exhibition games with the Angels.

So my body was burning up and I had to pitch six innings in Palm Springs. I told the coaches I couldn't do it, that I felt really bad. They said, "But Juan, the manager wants you to pitch." So I pitched six innings and they gave me a pill for my throat. Four days later, I had to pitch against the Padres in Yuma, Arizona. After that, the team sent me to see a doctor in Phoenix. He checked me out and told me what I thought I knew. "You have an infection in your throat," he said. He asked me if I had any allergy to penicillin and I said no, that I had taken penicillin before. So he gave me a shot, and the next day I had bumps on me as big and red as tomatoes, and a high fever.

That happened on a Wednesday. On Thursday I was burning up. On Friday I felt the same way. Saturday I was worse, and I called the doctor. It was so bad, they called a family doctor to make a house call to the clubhouse. The Giants were supposed to leave Phoenix the next day and go back to San Francisco. The season was supposed to start on the Tuesday after that.

When the doctor showed up he ran his finger over one of my legs, and then grabbed the other leg and did the same thing. He told the trainer he thought I had a reaction to the penicillin shot. The trainer again disagreed with a doctor's diagnosis, and he just gave me another shot.

We flew to San Francisco, but I still felt so sick. Alma and the kids were in the Dominican Republic, so I asked Ozzie Virgil to come to my house and stay with me. The next day I woke up and we were supposed to go to the ballpark, but I could barely sit up in bed and I couldn't move my arm. It was numb. I told Ozzie to call a doctor and get some transportation, an ambulance, to take me to the hospital. When I got there, they took me in and about 12 doctors had a meeting to talk about my case.

I was in the hospital for 10 days. After that I had to go back to the hospital every three months to get a cortisone shot. I was so weak I wondered if I could pitch all year. At one time I was taking 36 pills a day. I didn't start pitching until June.

That was the worst season of my career. I was 12–10, but my earned run average was 4.12. The sportswriters were saying that I was all done. A lot people told me that I could sue the doctor or the Giants, but I didn't feel that I could do that.

In between all my physical problems, I pitched some memorable games. On August 28, 1970, I won my 200th game. I beat the Pirates 5–1 at Candlestick Park. I had so many problems with my health that year, but when I won that game I told the sportswriters I was having fun again. I still count that win as a special one.

One of the writers gave me a ball to hold up with the No. 200 on it, and I think I still have it. A friend of mine also had a ring made up for me. I wasn't thinking about getting my 200th win leading up to it. I was just going to the mound hoping I would do a good job and win the game.

Another big game came the following year, in 1971. The manager then was Charlie Fox, and he told me I would be pitching the last game of the season. We were one game ahead of the Dodgers, and by that time they had added the National League Championship Series between the two division winners. We lost the second-to-last game of the season to San Diego, so it came down to us and the Dodgers on the last day. I felt good. I felt that I could pitch the last game against the Padres.

We went out to dinner the night before the game and I asked Ozzie Virgil to come up to my room and play cards. He had retired and was a coach then. We played gin rummy, just for fun. I said I didn't feel I could fall asleep and I wanted to play cards until I got so sleepy that I would just lie down. I told him to just close the door on the way out.

I knew how important the game was. It was on my mind, but unlike the early part of my career it wasn't as easy for me to fall asleep the night before I pitched. At four o'clock in the morning I told him, "Ozzie, you can go." He quit the game, I shut the door, and went to bed. At two o'clock in the afternoon, I got up. I didn't have breakfast. We were supposed to play at 7:15 that night so I had lunch.

The game was on September 30, 1971, and I was pitching a shutout until the fifth inning. We ended up winning 5–1, with Dave Kingman hitting a big home run for us. The only run the Padres scored was unearned because the runner got on when I was covering first base and dropped a perfect throw to my glove from second baseman Tito Fuentes. But we clinched the division that night with a 90–72 record. It was my 18th win of the season.

Under the new rules, we had to play the Pittsburgh Pirates for the right to go to the World Series. The Pirates beat us in the National League Championship Series, and then they beat the Baltimore Orioles to win the World Series. That was the year Roberto was the Most Valuable Player. I couldn't start the opener of the playoff series against the Pirates because I had pitched the last game of the season.

I didn't pitch until the third game of the series, when we played at Three Rivers Stadium in Pittsburgh. We lost 2–1. I gave up solo home runs to Bob Robertson and Richie Hebner. They only got four hits and we had just five. Bob Johnson was the winning pitcher. Their pitcher was supposed to be Nelson Briles, but he got a stomach ache and couldn't pitch and it worked out very well for them.

It had been nine years since we had been in the postseason. That's a long time, especially considering almost every year I thought we were going to make it. You always wish you could have won a World Series.

The Giants were always my team, from the first moment I came to the United States and went to spring training in Sanford, Florida, through the minors, and they were the team that gave me the chance to play in the majors in 1960.

But by the early 1970s we were not the same team that I knew. Felipe Alou had been traded to the Braves. Orlando had been traded to the Cardinals. Then, they even traded Willie Mays. Willie Mays! They traded him to the Mets.

I thought I would always be a Giant. I never thought I was going to play for another team. I kept hearing that Horace Stoneham needed money. It looked like they were having financial troubles. But in my heart I was a Giant and that's the team I wanted to stay with.

I loved the city of San Francisco and I loved the fans. I always had a good relationship with the San Francisco fans. It was my city, and they were my fans from the beginning.

CHAPTER 12

Becoming a Legend

*T*hroughout his major league career, Juan Marichal had a close rapport with the fans of San Francisco and those of the Dominican Republic. He was equally well received in his native home and his adopted home.

Several things contributed to his popularity. Most importantly, he was a winning pitcher, the ace of the Giants staff. Fans love a winner and a player they can count on. Winning games right from the start of his career with the Giants made Marichal popular, and he stayed popular. He was also a fan-friendly guy who signed autographs as often as he was asked. When he returned to the Dominican in the offseason, he reacted the same way to the people who greeted him warmly. He also treated the fans back home to some of his best work on the mound for Escogido. Returning to the Dominican winter league, Marichal was able to work on *his craft while entertaining the fans who had known him when he was young and continued to support him as an established major league pitcher.*

For a man in the public spotlight year-round who was always expected to be "on," Marichal was patient with adulation. He was cooperative with requests for his time, and he went out of his way to be open and accessible. Except for the inexplicable Johnny Roseboro incident, he never showed a temper.

Naturally, there were stresses and physical ailments, but Marichal knew his body better than anyone else. He knew what he had to do to keep himself sharp and in top-flight pitching mode. He was a genuinely outgoing person, so that made it easy for him to mix with crowds who adored him. He felt a responsibility to be there for the Giants fans who helped pay his salary, and for the Dominican fans who were his family and who rooted so hard for his success from a distance.

Once, after another hugely successful season in 1964, Marichal made his usual offseason trip to the Dominican, believing that he had fulfilled his vow to prove himself as one of the top pitchers in the sport—one whose name, as he had promised his mother, was often heard on the radio and television. Back at Laguna Verde, Marichal told his mother he was doing well as a pitcher in San Francisco.

Her response was direct. "That is all very good," she said, "but I wish you went to college."

Marichal never forgot how fortunate he was to make a living as a baseball player, and he never forgot where he came from. He wanted to offer payback to his Dominican supporters. He was keenly aware that not all of his countrymen were so lucky financially, and that even some of the best players did not get the same opportunities he had—or perhaps had not been able to capitalize on their chances.

However, Marichal did not have a crystal ball and could not have realized that his 18-win season in 1971, which helped propel the Giants to a division championship, would be his final grand moment in San Francisco. His ever-nagging back became a more serious problem, and he underwent surgery. In 1972, Marichal was 6–16, the worst record of his career, and in 1973 he finished 11–15.

Those were troubled times for the pitcher, and they proved to be his last two seasons pitching for the Giants. His love affair with the team, the city, and the fans was just as strong in his mind. After 13 years in the City by the Bay, he felt it was as much his home as the Dominican Republic.

There was one major difference. Marichal was so widely revered in the Dominican that he was constantly being approached to participate in presidential politics, either by endorsing a candidate or signing on to do some work for one party or another, or one candidate or another.

When the Time *magazine profile of Marichal came out during the Dominican election campaign of 1966, an anonymous voter was quoted as saying, "If Juan were running for president, it would be a landslide."*

FOR ME, IT WAS ALWAYS IMPORTANT TO SIGN AUTOGRAPHS. BOB FELLER, WHO JUST DIED AT 92, WAS A GREAT MAN WHO MAY have signed more autographs than anyone in history. Somebody told me he signed one million autographs. My friend Fergie Jenkins signs a lot of autographs. Somebody said he once signed 5,000 baseballs in a day for charity.

I went to Bob Feller's museum once with him in his hometown— Van Meter, Iowa—a very tiny place. Nice country. He showed me where he was born, and there was so much land. Even in his 90s, he still signed autographs nicely.

When I was playing we always stopped outside the stadium before we went home to sign autographs for the kids. Now it's big business, and some agents tell their players not to sign because the more they sign, the less value they have for an autograph. But it's hard to tell a kid that they have to pay for an autograph. Kids look up to you and you want to make friends with the fans. We never thought of charging for an autograph. It was something you did to be nice; it was important to be nice to the fans.

Now sometimes guys pay kids to stand in line and get the autographs for them, because they know players are more likely to sign for a little kid. It happens almost everywhere you go with a big crowd. But when I was playing, we just signed. I signed as many as I could.

Signing an autograph for a kid is such a small thing. How can you say no? And how can you say no when you are playing in that city for years and everyone treats you so well? My wife and I loved San Francisco. We got to go out everywhere on the town to fancy restaurants, to shows. People invited us everywhere.

Going back to the Dominican Republic was always a treat. People treated us so special. Dominicans love baseball so much, and if you are a good player they treat you like a hero. They want to do something for you. Back then, too, there were fewer of us. We really represented the whole country, and they wanted to see you when you came home.

My first year in the United States, in 1958, I won 21 games in the minors during the regular season and two more in the playoffs. So I ended up with 23 wins. At that time a coach in the Dominican started calling me "Juan 23." The people loved the name so much. They kept calling me "Juan 23" on the radio.

It was beautiful the way they treated me. It was a wonderful, wonderful feeling. Sometimes a lot of people would come to the airport to welcome me back. I think if that happens to any athlete, he has to feel good. I was very proud to come back home and have all those people waiting for me.

The only downside is that people had such big expectations. At first, I would pitch for Escogido when I came back. But when I became a starter in the big leagues and was throwing 300 innings a year, I couldn't do it. I needed to rest and save my arm.

My family and I began staying in San Francisco for most of the year. I would come back for just a month at a time with one of my girls. I knew that the fans in the Dominican wanted to see me, but it wasn't possible to pitch anymore. I had to protect myself. In 1965, I stopped playing in the winter. I had to, but it was hard because the people in the Dominican loved me and wanted to see me.

One of the first times I came back they brought me to see the mayor of Santo Domingo and they called it Juan Marichal Day. They gave me a big plaque. They had a big day for me. Everywhere I went, they had a big reception. There were lunches. There were banquets. Sometimes I had to make speeches. The Escogido ball club had a day and a night for Juan Marichal. One time they dedicated the winter tournament in my name. It was wonderful to see how everyone cared about me.

The president came to some of these events. He called me on the telephone. To be recognized by the president, that's a big deal, a big accomplishment.

In the United States one time, President George W. Bush had a lunch for all the Hall of Famers. I got to sit at a big table with the President of the United States and the First Lady. What more can you ask for than to have presidents recognize your accomplishments?

The Dominican Republic is a small country, so everyone knows all the athletes and what they do, especially in baseball. The United States is so much bigger, but even in the United States when I stayed there and lived there year-round I was invited to so many activities for charity, to raise money for schools, for kids. I had so much recognition I couldn't complain.

In 1963, I might have been *too* popular for a while. People in Latin America thought I was such a great pitcher that when I went to Venezuela with the Dominican Republic national team for the Caribbean Series, we got a phone call right away in my hotel that some people were going to kidnap me. They didn't want me to pitch against their team in Caracas.

They put guards all over that hotel, more than 50 guards. I was in one room, like 304, and the military was in 306 and 302. They checked up on who might be telephoning me. If somebody called my room the military grabbed the telephone in those neighboring rooms and they could listen to the conversation. It was like a spy movie. I was nervous. Then they got me transportation to the stadium with three military guys dressed in civilian clothes.

There was a military patrol car in front of us and another patrol car in the back. They didn't let me ride the team bus. The tournament was for five days, maybe a week, and we did this every day back and forth to the stadium.

At the stadium fans threw these fire things that exploded on the field like a bomb. They were more than a firecracker. Every time I was on the mound and one of those things exploded, man, I jumped. One day a phone call came from some people saying they were coming to get me, and they sent more military to the hotel. There were about 200 soldiers and they had machine guns and everything. But I went through with it. I pitched twice.

One game that I was pitching the other team got a man on first. The next batter hit the ball to right field, a base hit. Jesus Alou was playing right field and he threw the ball to third base. I was backing up third and the ball went over the third baseman's head, so I went back to the stands to field it and somebody threw something on top of my head and uniform. I thought it was beer. You know what it was? Pee. Urine. It was disgusting. They had to stop the game while I went into the clubhouse to change my uniform.

In some countries the feeling was that strong. I went to play in another city in Venezuela once, and while I was warming up in the bullpen somebody threw a rock and hit me in the ankle. My manager told the umpire and he told me to come to the mound and warm up out there. The fans were rooting for their team. Sometimes the fans in the Dominican, in Venezuela, or in Puerto Rico get a little— how do you say it—out of proportion. They want to win. They were trying to distract me. Sometimes people threw firecrackers that moved like snakes. You only see the fire and hear the whistle. Some threw shoes.

In 1965, there were real problems in my country, and the U.S. Marines came in. It was a delicate situation. A lot of my family was in the Dominican—my brothers, sisters, cousins, uncles. I was in San Francisco and it was very tough for an athlete to go to the mound every four days and keep his concentration on what he was supposed to do.

I kept getting phone calls from home, and I used to go to the Dominican consul's office in San Francisco to get the newspapers and see what was happening in the country. We saw some things on the TV news, but not that much. There was a photograph of Jesus Alou reading the newspaper from the Dominican.

A revolution was going on, and I had friends on both sides. There were people on both sides who wanted me to endorse someone from their side. It was easier for me to be in the United States and be Juan Marichal in San Francisco at that time. I didn't take any part. People wanted me to. I had been in the Air Force, and the Air Force and National Guard and police were fighting against civilians. I had a lot of friends on the civilian side. I didn't want to see people getting killed and fighting for something when they didn't even know what they were fighting for. It was a bad situation.

There was a general, a chief commander in the Air Force, who was a very good friend of mine. My wife's brother was a lieutenant. My wife's sister married another lieutenant, and her oldest sister married an officer who at that time was either a captain or a major. I had friends on both sides and I knew it was not good for the country. Then the United States sent in the Marines and people called it an invasion. They took that very hard.

When it was over, it was a new beginning for the country, but it took a long time for the people on the two sides to get together. The feeling on both sides was very tender after that.

One side wanted to bring back Juan Bosch as president. He had presided after Trujillo was assassinated. The other group was against it. Joaquin Balaguer, who had been president from 1960 to 1962, was living in exile in New York and Puerto Rico, and he returned to the Dominican in 1966. After he came back and took power, things stabilized. A group of his people came to see me in San Francisco when he was running for president. They wanted me to say something like, "Let's vote for a revolution with no blood and death." They were saying we should have a peaceful revolution. I did speak for him and he used my name. He said something like, Joaquin Balaguer is the Marichal of the palace, a nod to how I had been doing as a pitcher. He came back, was elected, and then was re-elected.

Some time later, after I retired from pitching, President Balaguer sent some people from his administration to meet with me in Miami. When I asked what they wanted from me, my compadre who arranged the meeting said President Balaguer wanted me to become "chief of the outfit." I said, "I don't know anything about politics." They said the president wanted to name me to the job because I was neutral in the public eye and I could bring the parties together. I told them I would not do anything without talking to my wife and children.

I talked it over with my wife and the first thing I said was, "No way I can accept that." I went to Balaguer's house to tell him myself, and when I walked in the door he told me to put my right hand up to be sworn in. Right there in his house. He asked me if I would accept and I said, "Yes sir." I took the job as chief of the political party for a certain district. I decided I couldn't refuse the president, and that job cost me a lot of money. I was the representative of the party in that district, so anyone who needed help came to me. You have to give help for a funeral, for a wedding, for people who needed food.

So I was in politics, but I wasn't truly in politics. They always wanted me to run for office, but I didn't want to. I was busy doing other things. Everybody loved me, and I wanted to keep it that way. I wanted to have everyone call me a friend, and when you run for office that's never the case.

At the time of the 1965 revolution, I had already established myself in baseball. I was at my peak, winning more than 20 games every year. By then I really knew what I was doing.

I had more confidence in myself, too. Not too many guys win 25 games. I knew the hitters and I knew all the counts to take advantage of. I was able to concentrate at a very high level. I might have had a few more wins in 1965 were it not for the Johnny Roseboro incident.

When you win 25 games, you come to spring training the following year and all you think about is being healthy so you can do it again. You know that if you're not hurt you are going to have another good year. And that's what happened. I had more confidence. I was more mature. My teammates were congratulating me all the time. They seemed to enjoy every minute of my good seasons. And so did the fans. I was winning three out of every four games. I remember reading that my winning percentage was so good that the gamblers in Las Vegas said I was the pitcher to bet on.

In the 1960s, I won more games than any other pitcher. I am very proud of that. I had six 20-win seasons.

Still, you always look for ways to get better. One year Fergie Jenkins came to the Dominican for winter ball and pitched for Escogido. He brought a lead ball to exercise his arm. I had been using a rubber ball that was very light, and I squeezed it a lot. I used to do a lot of exercises in the gym, but people told me not to lift heavy weights because it was bad for your arm. I agreed with that. A pitcher has to have a very flexible arm, and you need a very smooth motion. I used a rubber ball to strengthen my hand and fingers, but I didn't lift heavy weights because everyone said it would make me muscle-bound. Do you know another thing I did to make my fingers stronger? I used to type. I also did it because I wanted to learn how to type.

People do interesting things to try to become stronger. Somebody said it would help if you got a box or barrel of rice or beans and pushed your arm all the way down in it, and then pulled it back out. I did it maybe once or twice, but I don't know if that really helped. I looked at anything that might help make me stronger. I tried ice on my arm after a game. It never worked. I read about Sandy Koufax doing it every time he pitched. He got a big towel with ice and wrapped it around his arm. I said, "Okay, let me try that and see if it helps me." I did it and the next day my arm was all aching. It hurt so bad, I never did it again.

What worked for me after I pitched was to rub my arm, wrap a towel around it, step into the shower, and turn the hot water up as hot as I could take it and let it run for 15 or 20 minutes. Four days later I would be perfect to pitch again. That really helped.

When you are winning 75 percent of the time, everything is great. It looked like I was in a groove in those years. You get out to the mound, you feel comfortable, and you know you can do it. You feel like if you get a little help from your teammates, you are going to win every time you go out. If you don't get hitting support, you can end up losing. I lost some games 1–0 or 2–1, but I didn't lose too many.

In 1968 I won 26 games and lost nine. I felt like I could have won 35 games. With a little more help from my teammates, I think I could have won 30.

I never had a number in mind before the season. I just wanted to go out and pitch well. If you can do that, most of the time you come out on top. You're going to win. You might lose 1–0 or 2–1, but you win a lot. Winning is hard, though. You can win 15 by the all-star break and only win four more all season. That just shows it's not easy.

Sometimes you get in a groove and you win every game, and sometimes you pitch well and you can't win. Or you pitch well and get a no-decision. In baseball, you can never tell. The way they pitch now, no one is ever going to win 30 games again. They might not win 25. I started 40 games in 1963. Now they start 32 and they only go five or six innings. You don't have to win that many to make $25 million. The most I ever made was $140,000. That was pretty big, but guys like Manny Ramirez and Derek Jeter are making $20 million or more.

It's amazing what has happened with money in baseball. Some people today make that kind of money and they get crazy. They don't know what to do. If I made that kind of money when I was playing, maybe I would have gone crazy, too. I don't know. But I was happy with the way things happened. I had 16 years in the major leagues, created a beautiful family, and made beautiful friends. I'm very happy. I'm not jealous of today's players. If when I was playing someone came up to me and said 10 years from now, 15 years from now, people are going to make $25 million or $30 million to play baseball, I would have said, "You're crazy." But now I know it's not a dream.

I didn't have a goal that I wanted to do this or that in baseball, but winning my 200th game was a very special occasion. I won a total 243 games in the big leagues. What made me happy was that I won more games than any other Latin pitcher. I held that record for a long time until Dennis Martinez of Nicaragua broke it. He had 245 wins when he retired in 1998.

Dennis was a good pitcher, but I had a better earned run average and he never won 20 games in a season. He did throw a perfect game. But winning percentage counts, too. It took Dennis a long time. He pitched six or seven more years than I did. He played 23 years up until 1998, when he won four games with the Atlanta Braves to get the record, and he was 43 years old.

I talked to him after he broke my record. I congratulated him. I'm not jealous about numbers. One of these days someone might come along and win more. You never know. I thought Pedro Martinez might, but he won't now.

It made me feel good to have that record. I don't think it made me a hero. If people want to say something about me when I die, I want them to say, "He was so good." People know my name in the Dominican Republic, Puerto Rico, Venezuela, the United States, even Cuba. They are proud of me. I am one of them. Lots of people are proud of what I did.

Baseball is the No. 1 sport in these places, and it is because of the passion for the game. Latin people love baseball. They are so proud. Some people act like you are a god or they say you are a hero, but that is because they care so much about the game.

CHAPTER 13

Leaving Baseball

*J*uan *Marichal came up through the Giants organization and joined the big-league club in 1960. He pitched for the team into the 1970s. He and his family loved San Francisco. He thought he would pitch for the Giants forever.*

Things changed. Not only did Marichal, who was so dominant in the 1960s, begin to have physical problems that detracted from his statistics and performance on the mound, but all the other star teammates he had played with were gone, traded to other teams or retired.

Back surgery was a major factor in Marichal's 6–16 season of 1972. His earned run average was a respectable 3.71, but it was more than a run per game higher than it had been during his all-star seasons. In 1973, Marichal thought he would be fine, but his record was 11–15 with a 3.82 ERA.

Officials in the Giants organization thought he had reached the end of the line, and in a move that shocked the long-time ace of the franchise, Marichal was shipped to the Boston Red Sox before the 1974 season. He was 36 years old, but he felt he could still pitch, even though he was switching to the unfamiliar American League after an entire career spent in the National League.

Marichal went 5–1 for the Red Sox, but he did not get much of a chance to pitch. He started only nine games and appeared in just 11. His earned run average was a career-worst 4.87. He thought he was close to retirement after that 1974 season, but he decided to give it one more try. The surprise was that he chose to sign with the Los Angeles Dodgers, the old rivals against whom he had figured in so many showdown games.

These were not welcome moves for a man who was so committed to the city of San Francisco, whose family lived there year-round, and who had never felt he would play anywhere else. Like so many other players who are deeply passionate about the sport that had given them everything in life, Marichal did not want his major league career to end, and he was willing to work to regain the form that had made him an all-star.

Retirement loomed, but Marichal didn't want to admit it. The rhythm of the seasons he had followed for half his lifetime was about to be disrupted, and he was willing to do what it took to hold off the inevitable. He didn't know if he could keep playing, but he wanted to try for as long as he was able.

Most of the guys I played with and shared so much with over the years with the Giants were retired by 1974. I didn't feel like I was ready to retire.

I had had back surgery, but I thought I could recover and pitch like I used to. My back surgery was after the 1972 season, at the Stanford University Hospital. In 1973, I thought I was healthy enough to pitch like the old me, but I was never back to my old self. My body wasn't the same.

One of the things that got me ready to pitch again was lots of swimming in an indoor pool and walking in the water. I spent all that winter doing that in San Francisco. My legs were strong, but my back still wasn't right. When I had the surgery the doctor told me, "I don't know if you'll ever play baseball again, but you're going to be 80 percent better than you are now."

My back had started aching almost as soon as I got to the major leagues. It had held up for a long time, but during the 1972 season I was playing catch with Gaylord Perry and my back gave out. I had to lay down on the ground, and they carried me from there to the hospital. Another time I was hitting ground balls and I felt something go "pop" in there. I couldn't get up. So I went to the hospital again. I spent seven days in traction in a New York hospital.

I wanted to play that year for the Giants, but they sold my contract to the Red Sox. I was living in San Francisco during the offseason in 1973 and I got a phone call from Horace Stoneham in the Giants organization, telling me I was all through with the Giants and was going to the Red Sox.

I was very, very sad. I was a Giant all the way, all my life. Now I had to wear a new uniform. That looked weird to me, and I didn't feel very good about it. I went to spring training with the Red Sox.

In those days they were in Winter Haven, Florida. There were some Latinos with the team. Luis Tiant was there. Roger Moret, a pitcher from Puerto Rico, was there. Orlando Cepeda had been there as a designated hitter the year before. Orlando did well in Boston. He was named Comeback Player of the Year.

Boston gave me a good welcome. They thought I could help the team. I did, but I didn't play enough because I hurt my back again in June. They sent me to a hospital and I never came back to the team. It was just half a season. So that was it. I had thought I was going to be okay after my back surgery in 1972, but by 1974 I was starting to think I would never be okay again, at least as far as being an athlete—although part of me did not want to admit that.

One funny thing happened in Boston at the very beginning of the season, after we got there following spring training. A lot of us were living in a hotel right around the corner from the bleacher side of Fenway Park. It was early in the season, and they were having some of that famous New England weather. It was baseball season, and there was snow! When I woke up in the morning, I saw nothing but snow. It was beautiful. I have not seen snow many times in my life. It's supposed to be warm weather for baseball. I called up Luis Tiant, Mario Guerrero, Diego Segui, and Roger Moret and we went over to Fenway Park and built a very nice snowman.

Somebody was chewing gum, and with that gum we made a mouth that looked beautiful. It looked just like lipstick. Then we got one of Luis Tiant's cigars and we put it on the mouth and we took a picture of the snowman. Everybody posed for pictures as a group, and then one by one. When we were done, Guerrero came out with a bat and he destroyed it. He hit it in the head. There was snow flying all over the place.

One time, in all my years in San Francisco, we saw snow. They said it was the most snow, or the first time it snowed, in 35 years. But it was not like snow in the eastern part of the country. It was just a little bit. But my kids went wild. They started making snowballs and throwing them at each other.

Going 5–1 with the Red Sox, I was pitching pretty well. I wasn't great, but in one game against Oakland I gave up only three hits. Then my back started hurting again.

I knew something was wrong, anyway, because I used to be a good fielder on the mound. Anything that was hit close to me I could jump and grab very quickly. After the surgery the same balls I used to grab and get the man out at first base were coming by me, and when I reacted I was too late. I just saw the ball go past me. That's when I knew it was probably time to go.

It seemed to me that I still had all five of my pitches working, but that may have been in my head. As I got older my right shoulder hurt so much, and I asked the doctor why. He said, "I think you've got a little bit of arthritis." I think he's right. But back then, that was not the case. Now the other shoulder hurts, too. Maybe it's all old age.

I liked Boston. Carl Yastrzemski became a good friend. Luis Tiant was always a good guy. You know who was a great ballplayer? Dwight Evans. He was awesome. I think he was underrated, too. What a fielder.

I made a lot of friends in Boston, and I loved the food. I had seafood almost every night. One of my daughters, Yvette, went to Boston University and went through the communications school. People do love baseball in that town.

That was my only year with the Red Sox. I should have retired after that, and I was going to. My wife and kids wanted me to leave the game. They didn't mind me being at home. I made the decision to retire. I knew I was a different person since the surgery.

However, the Dodgers came to me and asked me to pitch for them, and I hesitated. I considered myself retired. But the Dodgers came to the Dominican to talk to me. Ralph Avila worked for the team and he came over. Manny Mota was with him. I told them, "No, I'm retired. I don't want to play baseball anymore."

I didn't think I should do it, but every athlete wants to give it one more try. We want to go out when we are playing well. People wondered how the Dodgers and their fans would accept me because of what had happened with Johnny Roseboro. But Johnny told everyone that it was okay with him, and that they should accept me. It was a nice thing to do.

I signed a contract with the Dodgers that said if I didn't think I was helping the club, I could retire at any time. I was overweight when I went to spring training, because I had been thinking I wasn't going to play. Then I lost 18 pounds in less than a month at spring training, so I got weak.

Early in the season, the Dodgers started me against Houston. I pitched three perfect innings, but the whole thing fell apart in the fourth. The Astros started hitting me all over the place. At my command, the team took me out of the game. I ended up getting the loss. Four or five days later, I faced Cincinnati. The same thing happened. Three good innings and, in the fourth, they started hitting line drives all over the place.

Walter Alston came out to the mound to get me. All the players were there. He said, "Juan, I think you've had enough. Go home and have a good night's sleep and see you tomorrow." I said, "Mr. Alston, I just retired." He said, "Oh, no, no, go home and relax. We'll talk about it tomorrow." And I repeated, "Mr. Alston, I retire."

After the game my wife was with me in the hotel and I told her what had happened, and that I was retiring. She was happy. Alma hugged me and said, "Oh, we're going home. We're going to be with our family." She was ready to go back to the Dominican.

The next day I got up and went to Peter O'Malley's office. He tried for about 45 minutes to convince me not to retire. I told him, "Mr. O'Malley, you know what the biggest problem is? I told my wife last night that I was retired. I can't go back to her and tell her that I'm not." He asked what I was going to do after I retired and I said, "I'm going to stay home and relax for some time."

We shook hands, I went to the clubhouse, and I said goodbye to all the players, Mr. Alston, and Tommy Lasorda, who was a coach. That was April 17, 1975. It was Yvette's birthday.

So I went to the Dodgers, but it really didn't work out and I never should have come back. I was in two games and my record was 0–1 with a 13.50 earned run average. I realized I couldn't pitch anymore. That's when I really retired.

After I left the ballpark I went to a music store and bought a guitar to take home as a birthday present for Yvette. I flew back to San Francisco and that was the end of my career as a pitcher.

It's hard to retire and give up what you have been doing for so long, but I was prepared. I had thought it through before the season, and I had the help of my family. I got used to winning, and when I started those two games for the Dodgers I knew that I was not going to be the same. I knew it right away. I was completely out of baseball, mentally. That's why I had gained the weight over the winter. I had decided already.

All the years I was playing I did not think about when I might retire. Year after year the sportswriters came up to me and asked,

"How many games do you think the team will win this year?" And they asked, "What is your goal for this year?" My answer was always the same. I said, "My goal is to be healthy." I knew if I was healthy, I was going to win some games.

I had some goals that I didn't attain. I wanted to win 300 games. I wanted to win the Cy Young Award. Even the years I won 25 games or 26 games, I didn't come close. Someone always had a great year. I was the wrong player at the wrong time. In 1968, when I won 26 games, Bob Gibson had one of the best seasons of any pitcher in history. He came out with a 1.12 earned run average and 13 shutouts, and he won 22 games. In 1964, when there was only one winner for both leagues, Dean Chance won the award. He had 20 wins and a 1.65 earned run average for the Angels.

In 1967, I was not well and I finished 14–10. My teammate Mike McCormick finished 22–10 and he won the Cy Young Award. I was 12–7 going into the All-Star Game, but I hurt my left leg. When I got to a doctor in Los Angeles he told the Giants, "If you keep pitching him, you are going to ruin his career." I won only two more games after the break.

After I retired, I stayed in San Francisco for two years and did nothing but watch baseball and play golf. I took golf lessons from Chi Chi Rodriguez from Puerto Rico, who was selected for the golf Hall of Fame. Then I used to play with Felipe and Matty Alou. It was very hot out in the summer when we played, and whoever lost had to buy watermelon so we could cool off. Matty was the best one. When he was a kid he was a caddy at the Santo Domingo Country Club, so he knew how to play. Between Felipe and I, sometimes he was last and sometimes I was last, but Matty never had to pay for watermelon. It was not big stakes. We didn't want anybody's money. We played just for friendship.

The worst thing was that I didn't have too many friends to play with. I was retired, and my friends were working so they were busy on weekdays. I spent the rest of my time watching baseball for two years. I really missed the game so much. But I didn't miss the traveling. I enjoyed being with my kids because I had lost so much time with them when they were growing up. I lost many years. Maybe I only saw them half the year, between spring training and traveling. Now I was home all the time. That was fun.

I got an offer from the Giants about six months after I retired. The first offer was to be a scout in the Dominican. The man who signed me back in the 1950s, Horacio Martinez, had become a compadre. He baptized one of my daughters. I didn't want to take his job away. So I told the Giants no. I said, "Horacio has been your scout for many years, so I don't think it's fair for me to take his place."

After two years of watching baseball on TV and playing golf, one day I was lying on the floor watching a game and Alma said, "Do you want to go back home?" It sounded just right. I never reacted so fast. Before she could finish the words "back home," I think I was packing.

We moved the whole family back to the Dominican. We worked really hard and did research and found a great school for the kids, and then they had a hard time adjusting to the culture. They wanted to go back to San Francisco. So my wife said, "Let's go back to San Francisco."

At that time I went into the insurance business. A compadre of mine and I got together and opened a company. He was the president and I was the vice president. I did that for five or six years. I was happy doing that.

When we decided to go back to San Francisco, we decided not to live in the city. Alma was hard to please, but after looking for a long time we finally found a house in a really nice neighborhood outside the city. While we were standing at this place that we both liked, a man in a pickup truck drove up, took out a sign, and with a hammer he put it up. It said, "Sold." And just like that, we went back to the Dominican.

We had two more kids there. Charlene was born in 1980 and Juanchi—Juan Antonio—was born in 1981. We also found, in 1979, the house we still have, but it hadn't been built yet. It took two years for it to be completely finished and for us to get all moved in. My wife was changing this and changing that. She would say, "I don't like this" or "I don't like that." Some of my friends said, "Juan, if you don't move in, you're never going to finish the house." Of course there was a heavy, heavy rain the day we moved in.

We still had things in San Francisco. For a long time we had two places. In 1989, we were back in the Bay Area for the World Series between San Francisco and Oakland. That was the year they had the earthquake that interrupted the World Series for days. What a terrible tragedy that was.

It was October 17, 1989. The Loma Prieta earthquake hit just after five o'clock in the afternoon. A lot of people were just getting to Candlestick Park for the third game of the World Series. It was scary. Alma and I were walking down the stairs to our field box when the stadium started shaking. I was getting dizzy. I was getting sick. I stopped and I was holding her by the arm. I said, "What's happening?"

Alma said, "I don't know what's happening, but I see everything moving." There was all this noise and shaking. The earthquake lasted 10 or 15 seconds, but it seemed like longer when you were in it. After it was over, she said, "You can sell everything we have here. I'm not coming back."

That made us think of the Dominican, and how there is nothing like home. But a year later the Athletics were back in the World Series against the Cincinnati Reds, and she came back with me to visit.

CHAPTER 14

A Hall of Famer

*W*hen Juan Marichal retired early in the 1975
season, he had compiled a spectacular pitching
*résumé. The Dominican hurler had broken in with the
Giants midway through the 1960 season and finished his
career with the Dodgers less than a month into the 1975 slate.
Baseball records count that as 16 years, although Marichal
mostly refers to his career as lasting 15 years in the majors.*

*Marichal's final record was 243–142. More than a
100-game discrepancy in wins over losses is a rare achieve-
ment for any pitcher, and at the time his 243 victories
were the most in history by a Latin American pitcher.
That record stood for 23 years, until Nicaraguan Dennis
Martinez surpassed it, amassing 245.*

*Marichal's career earned run average of 2.89 is one of
the best of the last several decades. He pitched a workhorse*

3,507 innings and completed 244 games. Although not regarded as a strikeout pitcher, Marichal fanned 2,303 batters, six times topping the 200-strikeout mark in a season. His ratio of strikeouts to walks—a tribute to his trademark control—was 5.9 to 1. Marichal walked about one hitter for every five innings he pitched. He was a 10-time all-star.

After Marichal won his 200th career game in 1970, he said the triumph renewed him and made him feel as if he could go on winning games for years. He was mistaken. The allergic reaction to the penicillin and his deteriorating back shut him down more quickly than anticipated.

When Marichal gave his farewell-to-baseball press conference in Los Angeles, he did so resignedly, but with the knowledge that it was the proper time to say goodbye. "It could only have gotten worse," he said. "Retiring is the only thing for me to do."

Marichal's retirement in 1975 started the clock ticking on his Hall of Fame eligibility. Players must wait five years after their departure from the sport before they can appear on the Hall of Fame's selection ballot.

A man with Marichal's achievements these days would almost surely be a first-ballot Hall of Famer. However, elections came and went in the early 1980s, and Marichal was passed over.

Some theories surfaced about why he was excluded. One of them was that Marichal was out of the limelight. Another explanation was that Latin ballplayers simply did not get commensurate attention for their accomplishments. But the biggest issue for many voters (although it was not widely admitted) was the Johnny Roseboro incident. Some baseball writers weighed that mistake against Marichal's mound magic and held back their vote to include him in the Hall.

Marichal himself brought the matter to the forefront after his vote totals came up short twice, saying that was why he was being kept out. "It is the only thing I regret in my life," he said.

Marichal had looked at the records, and at that time, he had more wins than 32 of the 42 pitchers in the Hall of Fame. That apparently didn't matter to the voters. The Cardinals' Bob Gibson was once told he was the best pitcher in the National League, but Gibson said he wasn't, contending that he was second to Juan Marichal. Even in the early 1970s, when Marichal seemed to be losing his stuff, reliever Don McMahon said he was still one of the two or three best pitchers in the league. Finally, Roseboro issued a statement of support, saying that the bat incident should not be held against the pitcher.

In 1983, eight years after his retirement and three years after his eligibility began, common sense prevailed and Marichal received the necessary votes to be enshrined in Cooperstown. On a very hot day in August, an admittedly nervous Marichal was inducted into the National Baseball Hall of Fame.

During the years when I didn't get into the Hall of Fame, people talked to me a lot about it. They would tell me, "You should be in the Hall of Fame."

I was thinking about how I had won 20 games six times and had never won the Cy Young Award. People used to say that, too, that I should have won a Cy Young Award. I was thinking the same kind of thing about the Hall of Fame. I didn't pay too much attention at first. But then I started comparing my record with other pitchers' numbers and I said, "Well, my numbers are better than that."

You look at the earned run average and you look at how many games I am over .500—my winning percentage was .631, and not too many pitchers have that.

Each time they voted I thought, maybe now. When I didn't get elected I wasn't too sure what would happen. I wasn't campaigning so much. I started to think that if it happens, welcome. If it doesn't happen, I won't be too mad about it. Things happen. If they didn't give me a plaque or a trophy, I still wanted to be happy with my friends and family.

That was a long time ago, and maybe if 20 years had passed and they didn't elect me I might have felt differently about it. The more I learned about the Hall of Fame and about the people who had been in there for many years, then yes, if I had not been elected I might have been upset.

At that time, the only Latin player in the Hall of Fame was Roberto Clemente. After he died in 1972, they put him in right away. They didn't wait the five years.

Finally, one day, I got a phone call from an official from the Baseball Writers Association, Jack Lang. He called to tell me that I was elected to the Hall of Fame. I was the first Latin player to be elected by the voters through the regular procedures.

Jack gave me the news, but he said I couldn't tell anybody. They were going to fly me to New York for a press conference right away. When I got off the phone I called my wife in the Dominican right away to tell her the news. I told her she could not tell anyone so it didn't spread all over the island. It was hard to hold it in. I didn't tell my kids until the official announcement. I didn't know if I could hold the news in, but I followed the rules. I learned that in the Air Force. Maybe my wife told her sister and mother and father. I don't know. I didn't ask.

I flew to New York, and they held a press conference at a big hotel. That was beautiful. Also at the press conference was Brooks Robinson of the Orioles, a player I respected very much and who made it in on his first year on the ballot. Walter Alston, the Dodgers manager, and George Kell, a third baseman in the 1940s and 1950s, were elected that same year by the Veterans Committee.

For a while I had not worried about getting into the Hall of Fame, but I had plenty of time to think about how I would feel when it finally happened. I hugged Alma and told her how happy I was. I thanked God. So many players go through the game and never have the experiences I did. I was one of the lucky players, a small number, who reach the Hall of Fame. I thanked God for helping me in my career and giving me the opportunity to play a beautiful sport.

When I made my speech at the Hall of Fame in Cooperstown that summer, I told the people that the plaque did not belong to Juan Marichal, but it belonged to all of Latin America. It belonged to my country, to Latin America, and to all Latin ballplayers.

If you think about it, there were hardly any Latin ballplayers until the 1950s. Then we had some more come to play in the majors during the 1960s, and more and more in the decades after that. Only a small percentage of these players would be good enough to get into the Hall of Fame. They play for a lot of years and then they have to wait five years after they retire, at least, to be considered. So even though there are hundreds of Latin American players now, there are still not very many in the Hall of Fame.

Roberto Alomar, who is from Puerto Rico, was elected in 2011, and before that the last Latin from the majors to be inducted in the Hall of Fame was Tony Perez, from Cuba, in 2000. My old friend Orlando Cepeda had to wait until 1999 to get a place in the Hall of Fame—25 years after he stopped playing. Minnie Minoso was one of the first players from Cuba to make it big in the majors, but he has not been elected to the Hall of Fame. I think he should be in there, too.

Although I am very proud of my country, I always felt I was representing more than just the Dominican. It wasn't just the Dominican Republic that was rooting for Juan Marichal, either. It was all Latin American baseball fans. I felt I had a responsibility to be a role model to all of them. I thought about that a lot. Sometimes I said to my wife, "I have to behave in a certain way, maybe not because I want to do it, but because I have to do it." I should do it, I used to say. That was like a joke to her, that I have a responsibility to act a certain way because people think so highly of me. I have to let them know they are not wrong. Of course, your wife doesn't look at you that way. She knows you are a human being who can make mistakes. But that role meant something to me, to be one of those people Dominican or Latin people looked up to.

I worked hard to lead a healthy lifestyle. When I was pitching on the road I went to bed early. I didn't stay out late. I didn't like disco. I felt it was very bad for my eyes with all the smoke in clubs.

And I didn't like to be in a place where you could not talk because of all the noise. I could go to a small party. I could go to a wedding. I could go out to dinner. But to go to a disco, I couldn't stand it. I liked to go to shows with a good singer or actor, but I couldn't stand the smoke in those places. Now they ban the smoke, but before people smoked everywhere.

I did not smoke. I did not drink, except maybe two beers on a hot day. Before I retired, every time we played in Houston the Dominican consul would give me two cases of whiskey to take back to San Francisco. I had learned a little bit about drinking since I was in the Air Force, but I never had more than one or two. I wasn't a good drinker. I still thought about how if you take a drink and you have to make a face because of how it tastes and feels, it can't be good for you.

People say there are all these temptations, but in my life I put God first, my family second, and my profession third.

One time in the Air Force, a group of guys went out drinking and the coach found out right away. He worked all of us so hard that the next day some of the guys were throwing up. He wanted everyone to give up. He kept running us and I kept telling myself, "Don't give up." A couple of the guys had to go to the clinic. I didn't talk to that coach for a week.

After that week passed, he sat me down to give me a lecture about my future and what I could become. He kept pointing at different players, one at a time. He said, "See that guy over there? He's a good third baseman. But he's 24. You see that guy over there? He's a very good shortstop. But he's 27." I was 19. He said, "You don't know what you can be in the future. You could have a great career as a pitcher, but you have to be careful. You have to take care of yourself.

You can be those guys' friend, but don't go out with them." And that was pretty much how it was for the rest of my baseball career. I was friends with guys on the team, but I didn't go out at night to clubs with them. I was not that type. I used to see guys come to the stadium drunk and play. I don't know how they could do it.

Staying away from that really helped my career. That's why I say I sacrificed. After I got to the major leagues, I wasn't satisfied with just being there. I wanted to be one of the best. The only way you can do that is to take good care of yourself.

I also never wanted to do anything that would reflect badly on Latin players. When I first came to the majors, not everyone in the sport welcomed us. One reason was the language barrier. The other was the color of our skin. Time passed and more and more Latinos were able to play and compete and be treated fairly.

After I retired, one of the most amazing things that showed me how much times had changed was when Fernando Valenzuela broke in with the Dodgers in 1981. He came from nowhere and became a star so fast. He was Mexican, and nobody cared. He spoke Spanish, and nobody cared. Everyone loved him.

One minute nobody knew who Fernando was. Then he won all those games. He had a pitching style where he closed his eyes and seemed to be looking to the heavens. He was so popular, especially in Latin America. Players could go their whole lives and not be that popular. But he attracted people. He was an exciting player, and a winner. He sold out stadiums everywhere. I think Fernando was what is called a "crossover star." He was someone who represented change.

Fernando had everything on his side at the right time. He also came to the right place. Maybe if he had come up in St. Louis, there would not have been "Fernando Mania." He was in Los Angeles, where there are so many people of Latin descent, especially Mexicans. It was awesome to see.

That was a big step for Latin players. I'm not sure if anyone would have loved a Latin player so much in 1958, no matter what he did. Even the great Roberto Clemente, who won all those batting titles and played in all those All-Star Games in the 1960s, was not so popular. People tried to call him "Bob" and accused him of faking injuries.

I remember my first game in the major leagues. I remember the first time I was elected to an All-Star Game. I remember the 1962 World Series. I have so many memories, but that day in Cooperstown was something else. It was the greatest day of my baseball career. Number two was the day I found out I was going into the Hall of Fame.

Cooperstown is a beautiful place, and I love going back each year for the ceremonies. One time I said to Alma, "This is a beautiful place to retire." She looked at me and said, "Well, if you do that, I think you're going to retire by yourself." She does not like snow and winter.

I was very nervous for the press conference in New York, but I was very excited. I had waited eight years. After the press conference I flew back to the Dominican, and by then everybody knew. There were so many people waiting at the airport—sportswriters, family, friends. I will never forget walking down the stairs to the terminal. The airport was full of people. They made me stop right on top of the stairs to take pictures.

We had a press conference at the airport and then I had to go, because President Jorge Blanco was waiting for me. I have a picture of when he welcomed me to the presidential palace and congratulated me. That was a big day in the Dominican. Alma and I went out to dinner with friends. I received recognition from the mayor of the city and from a few other places. It was a great event everywhere. Everyone wanted to make me happy, and they did.

My wife and kids and a lot of friends came from the Dominican for the Hall of Fame induction ceremony in Cooperstown. Pepe Copello, Billy Alvarez, and their wives, these were my compadres. We have been friends forever.

It was so hot that day, I was sweating. But I also had a few tears. I was never nervous when I saw Hank Aaron or Roberto Clemente or Orlando Cepeda at the plate, but that day, oh my God. It felt completely different than anything else I had done.

You think for a long time about what it will be like. Months pass between the time they call you and the time you go to Cooperstown. You think about how you are going to compose yourself. You want it to happen right away, and you want to control your emotions.

It means so much to an athlete to be part of that group. When you are playing, you never think you are going to be in the Hall of Fame next to those guys with the famous names. After you get in, you learn more about the different people who got in that you played with or against. You feel so happy to see those guys get in, because you know how happy you were when you got in. It's a wonderful feeling, and every year it's a beautiful get-together. The commissioner is there, the president of the museum and all the old friends. That's something. Sometimes you don't believe that you are there, that you are one of those guys.

There are guys about whom I ask myself why they never made it into the Hall of Fame. Guys like Buck O'Neil, from the Negro

Leagues. I never come up with an answer. Every year I sat down and talked with Buck O'Neil. I remember the way he dressed, so sharp. I just felt so bad he didn't get in. He should be in there. I bet one of these days they will put him in. They should have done it while he was still alive.

When you realize that you belong in the Hall with all those great players, you want to be there every time somebody new gets in. I don't want to miss a year. I feel like I want to welcome the new guys coming in, and I want to be together with every member. I wish someday all the living members would come. It's hard to get them all there, but someday I wish we could get a picture of everybody.

I also got friendly with players from the past whom I would not have seen any other way, and I became better friends with players from my time whom I did not know well when we played. I remember when Catfish Hunter got in and I invited him to the Dominican to participate in the Juan Marichal Golf Classic. I was sad when he passed away. Willie Stargell, what a sweet man. He was so good and it was hard to see a guy at that age, 61, pass away. Another person I always got together with was Robin Roberts. He died in 2010.

Joe DiMaggio came to the Dominican once and we got together. Ted Williams came to a fishing tournament. I really enjoyed talking with Ted. He talked nothing but baseball. A great man. In 1999, I was at Fenway Park for the All-Star Game when he came back. Everybody wanted to get a picture taken with Ted Williams in the golf cart. He was the type of man you just wanted to be around, just to listen to him. He was one of the best. That was one of my favorite days at the All-Star Game.

Another time, at the World Series in 2005, there was a ceremony for a Latin Legends team. The fans voted on it, and I made the team.

That was a very special ceremony. So many great Latin players together—Mariano Rivera, Alex Rodriguez, Rod Carew, Luis Tiant, Tony Perez, Pedro Martinez.

We got a chance to talk some, but we didn't have much time because it was at the World Series. One of the jokers was Ozzie Guillen, manager of the White Sox. He is from Venezuela, and man can he talk. I read a lot of stories where people criticize him, but I think I would have loved to play for him. He tells the truth. He says the things he feels. He doesn't hold things back, and he is very funny. I like him very much.

Being named a Latin Legend was amazing. It is always good to be remembered.

CHAPTER 15

Back in Baseball

After Juan Marichal put down his glove and retired as a pitcher, he stepped back from the spotlight and relaxed with a two-year decompression, removed from baseball except for watching games on television. He split his time between the United States and the Dominican, threw himself into his new insurance business, and spent time with his growing children.

His induction into the Baseball Hall of Fame in 1983 put him back into the limelight. In the 25 years since Marichal had first signed with the Giants and went off to play minor league baseball in Michigan City, Indiana, the sport and American society had changed.

No one would be foolish enough to say that there was 100 percent racial harmony in America during the 1980s, but the country's race relations had improved drastically.

The Hispanic population was growing. Whereas once it was found only in exotic specialty restaurants, Mexican food was easily obtainable. Taco Bell was like the second coming of McDonald's, and nobody thought twice about it.

Baseball, which had once been a shamefully exclusionary sport, refusing to allow dark-skinned players into organized professional ball—whether blacks from New York, Philadelphia, or Chicago, or Latins from the Dominican, Venezuela, or Puerto Rico—was much more of an equal-opportunity employer. Even those who previously believed there was an unwritten quota of the number of Latins allowed on a major league roster were starting to feel that all players were given the same looks, and that the game on the field had truly become a meritocracy.

In the 1950s, even the best Latin players had to be lucky to get noticed and sign a major league deal. There were several reasons why Roberto Clemente was such a hero to Latin players. It was not merely his excellence on the field or his proud demeanor that reminded fans and American sportswriters of his allegiance to his heritage, but it was also his timing. In the late 1950s, when Clemente became a star, he was one of the only Latin players that a young player with aspirations could look to as a role model. Orlando Cepeda, Juan Marichal, and other all-stars were in the next wave. They all helped jump-start a movement.

In the 1950s, only a handful of teams were actively scouting in the Caribbean Basin and Latin America. The Washington Senators and Pittsburgh Pirates took the initiative, and then the San Francisco Giants and the

Los Angeles Dodgers followed suit. By the mid-1980s, it was apparent that Latin America was a great, fairly untapped region for talent. More and more Latin players were reaching the majors. A series of Venezuelan infielders stamped the shortstop position as uniquely "owned" by that country. Chico Carrasquel begat Luis Aparicio, who begat Davey Concepcion, who begat Ozzie Guillen. Dominicans were also filling up roster spots.

Although there seemed to be a Latin American specialization in middle infielders for a while, it soon became obvious that there were no limitations. Name the position, and your next third baseman or left fielder might be signed by a scout roaming never-before investigated backwoods sandlots. Hall of Famer Rod Carew came from Panama. Hungry Cubans defected from Fidel Castro's island.

The smartest major league teams opened on-site skills schools in Latin American nations. They signed young players and developed them. Teams learned that even a minimal signing bonus could transform not only a poor player's life but also his family's economic status for all time. Unlike the United States, where many of the best athletes were gravitating to basketball, football, and other pursuits, the best athletes in many Latin countries played baseball.

After being away from his sport for nearly a decade, Juan Marichal picked up his telephone one day and soon after found himself leading a new life in baseball.

ONE DAY IN 1984 I RECEIVED A TELEPHONE CALL FROM THE OAKLAND ATHLETICS ASKING ME IF I WANTED TO WORK AS director of scouting for Latin America for them. The first thing I asked was who recommended me. I found out it was Bill Rigney, the old manager of the Giants. He was the one who sent me down to Tacoma, then got fired before I was brought up to the majors. Actually, he said he wanted to keep me with the Giants, but Horace Stoneham had overruled him.

I accepted the job with Oakland and I spent 14 seasons working for the A's as scouting director. Before I started with the A's, a lot of people asked me why I wasn't working for the Giants. I didn't have an answer. Maybe they wanted to talk to me after a while, but by then I was an employee of the Oakland A's. I was private property. It seemed strange to not be working for the Giants, even if Oakland was in the same area. But they were in the American League, so we were not competing with the Giants really. At least not directly. I didn't take it that hard. I was paid very well with that organization. Sandy Alderson hired me. He was general manager then, and later he became president of the team.

The first thing I did as a scout for the A's was sign kids for the organization from the Dominican. Then one time I told my bosses in Oakland how important it would be to build a baseball academy in the country. The Toronto Blue Jays had built the first one, and the Dodgers had one that was working very well. Even a club from Japan built an academy in the Dominican.

The A's agreed and gave me money to buy the land. We hired an architect and engineer to design the project. We built a beautiful academy about an hour north of Santo Domingo. Before that, as soon as we signed young players, we sent them to the United States.

Most of them weren't prepared for that. They were 16 and 17 years old. They didn't speak English. They weren't old enough to be on their own.

The Academy opened in the early 1990s. When we signed the kids, we kept them at the academy for two years. They worked out in the gymnasium, and you couldn't even recognize them they put on so much muscle. We fed them and taught them the fundamentals of baseball. Of the first 100 players I signed, 34 made it to the big leagues. Miguel Tejada, Luis Polonia, Tony Batista, and Miguel Olivo were some of the first ones. That was both before and after the academy started.

Tejada was the best player I signed for the A's. He has been in the majors since 1997, has made six all-star teams and won the American League Most Valuable Player Award in 2002. Tony Batista, a very poor teenager when I signed him, was good, but he was also very lucky. Everywhere he went, he made great money, including Arizona and Japan. He is still playing in the Dominican.

Once we opened the academy, the A's found out right away that the players developed more quickly in two years at the academy than in two years in the United States. That's why there are so many academies now. Just about every team has its own Latin academy now. You won't believe how much money comes from the United States to the academies and how that helps the local economy.

When I started as scouting director, I had a lot of scouts working for me. They traveled around the whole country to see kids play. They were looking at players about 16 years old playing amateur ball. It wasn't too organized. On one Sunday you might see one guy play here and another guy play here, on sandlots.

We had a rule that even before you sign them, you give them a tryout of sorts. You bring a player to the academy and you have an agreement with them for one month. After a month, you can either sign them for the A's, let them go, or get permission for another month to watch them. If you don't sign them after two months, you have to let them go. Sometimes someone else signs them. If they were at least 16, they could be signed and live at the academy for two years before going to the United States.

The first thing I did when I was scouting was go to the parents, since the kids were minors. You can't go and talk to a kid about signing without the permission of a parent. We went to their homes.

Some people were living in apartments. Some were living in small homes in the country. Many were very poor families. About 95 percent of the young players came from very poor families. One of the worst situations we found is when these kids were not even in school.

One thing that happened in the Dominican when lots of teams were scouting is that they started thinking about signing only the youngest players with potential. They wanted players who were 16, not 19. Sometimes if the player was 19, they said he was too old. Before I took over, the scout in my position in the Dominican used to sign players in my country who were 18, 19, and 20. They used their real ages. Now a kid 18, 19, or 20 doesn't have a chance. So they started changing their names and birth certificates.

Ages were being faked, since for them this was a once-in-a-lifetime chance. They said they were 16 when they were really 18 or 19. A *buscon*, a middle man, would become an agent for a player and his family and would tell the kid to change his age, name, or both, and tell him it was the only way he was going to get signed. The kids are not going to say no. These young players see an opportunity to become rich in the United States.

It made me feel bad when I signed a kid and people would say, "Oh, we never know his real age or his name because he is a Dominican player." It was not as big an issue when I first started, because we didn't pay that much money. When teams started paying more money, it became a problem. The biggest bonus I gave to a kid at that time was $25,000. Tejada, Polonia, Batista all got $5,000. Now kids get $3 million or $4 million. Things have changed a lot.

In the Dominican, you have to have an ID like a birth certificate to cash a check. Well, if they are not real birth certificates, those players are breaking the law. We have to get together with the majors to work out a different way.

Once we got permission from parents to take the kids to the academy, they lived there for a month in a dormitory. We had room for 80 kids at a time. They played a lot of baseball and they ate well. We had a professional chef for nutrition. They had teachers at the academy for schooling. If a kid lived outside of Santo Domingo, he could go home on weekends. Everyone is excited to see their kid get a chance.

I have a nephew, Chago, who was a really good scout. He had vision. He would tell me, "I like that kid." And I asked him what he saw in him. Chago said, "Well, if that kid can put on maybe 20 more pounds he's going to have more power." Or he would say he would be able to throw harder. He could see those things, project into the future, what that kid would be like when he grew a few more inches or got taller. I learned a lot. I made some mistakes with players. Some guys I could have signed and didn't. Adrian Beltre, I could have signed him.

Sometimes I might have liked a kid, but the team sent someone from the United States and they didn't want to sign him. They came to the Dominican to evaluate players. We didn't sign Raul Mondesi because someone came from the United States and said, "He's a little bit fat. He is too chubby." But he was a great player right from the beginning. He was fast, with a good arm, a good hitter. He had everything. They were worried he was going to gain more weight. Instead, he really helped the Dodgers.

Some of the other scouts like my nephew could sign a player, but sometimes they called me and said I had to go to a specific house. The parents didn't believe I was involved and they wanted to see me for themselves. I used to go with Charo because of my name.

One of the most difficult situations when I was growing up was arguing with my mother about playing baseball instead of going to school. When I saw kids, I didn't want them to be like me. I wanted them to go to school and play baseball, too, and I told them they could do both.

We signed a lot of good players, but sometimes you sign one and they never develop. You make mistakes. I signed a catcher by the name of Jorge Brito. He was a good defensive catcher with a good body, but he could never hit much. He didn't last long in the majors, two years as a backup with the Colorado Rockies. But he made it.

When he came to Santo Domingo as a teen, the first thing he said was, "I want to sign right away." Then he said he wanted to go to high school. He wanted to graduate. He practiced during the daytime and we sent him to school at night and he graduated. I wanted every kid to graduate.

When I went to the parents' house, every kid was excited. They were all excited that I was there. The only thing the kids really wanted, though, was to be signed. Sometimes when they saw me they were impressed or shocked, but these were kids with nothing. You had to give them shoes. You had to give them clothes. They had nothing. Sometimes as soon as you saw a kid you knew that he wasn't eating enough. You could tell.

They came to live at the academy and after a month you had to tell some of them that we were not going to sign them. That was the worst part. I knew they were not eating and the future of the family might depend on how well they played. And I had to turn many of them back. That was very hard. Sometimes we let kids go and we talked to scouts from other teams to see if they wanted to bring them to their academies. Some of them did get to go and some of them got signed.

I worried about them, and it was so hard to send them away. They are adults now, and when I see some of them they come up to me and say, "Do you remember me? I was at your school at one time." I ask how they feel and how are they doing. If they say, "I've got a good job," I say, "Well, I'm happy for you." But not all of them have the same luck.

Sometimes when I had to send a kid back home he would sit across from me at the table and plead with me for another chance. Sometimes they were crying. One of the players in the academy cried the day he left because he wanted to be signed by me. But he signed with somebody else and he made it.

That's the sad part of the job. Sometimes it was so hard for me to let somebody go, I had to have my nephew do it. He had to do the dirty job if it was too hard for me to take because I really liked a kid.

If you weren't going to send a kid to a team in the minors in the United States after two years, you had to release him. The rule is that they have to be a free agent after two years. You can't keep them forever to keep them away from other teams.

Before the academies, when kids got sent to the minors, it could be very hard for them. They might not have a teammate who spoke Spanish. If they stayed at the academy for two years, they learned English, how to eat in the United States, and how to understand some of American society and culture. I know some people think that when these kids get to the United States all they eat is McDonald's, but now they go to those places where it is an all-you-can-eat buffet for, I don't know, $5.99. It's unbelievable what some of these kids can eat.

There are so many differences compared with when I first went to the Giants. The academies are a big help for the young players. Not every one of them is going to find a Mrs. Johnson to help them like I did. In the Rookie League or Class A they get meal money, but I don't like that they don't feed themselves properly. They might spend the money on something else like fancy tennis shoes, or jeans or a girl, and they still go to McDonald's a lot of the time. One pitcher I signed way back who was a really good prospect, all he did with his meal money was eat spaghetti and bread. He got so big he couldn't pitch.

So many kids play baseball in the Dominican. It's the national sport. That's true in many Latin American countries. The situation is much different than when I was a kid. We always loved baseball, but it was hard to get a chance to play in the United States. There was still discrimination when I went to the Giants, but it's so much better now. There is so much more opportunity.

All through the years after I broke into the majors, the sport was getting better and better in the Dominican. The more Latin players who played in the majors, the more role models there were for other Latin players just starting out. I feel sorry for the people I know who could have been in the big leagues had it been different back then. My friend Diomedes Olivo, he didn't play until he was 42. He could have played when he was much younger. And his brother Chi Chi. Who knows what they could have been? Maybe they could have been in the Hall of Fame. Orlando Cepeda's father, Perucho, was so good. In the Negro Leagues you could find a lot of guys who might have been stars in the majors, and some of them were Latin.

While the Giants and Pirates had Latin players, some teams had none. We noticed. We might make comments to each other, but never to the white players. We used to say some players in the minors who were Latin or black belonged in the majors, but we didn't think they were going to make it because they were with teams that had a quota or didn't want dark-skinned players at all.

Nobody thinks that way now. When an organization comes to the Dominican Republic, or to Venezuela or Puerto Rico, they pay a lot of money to some of these kids. They want to develop players to become major leaguers. Success changes things. If someone can become a good player, he's going to play somewhere. It doesn't matter what color his skin is, or his race. Right now we have about 100 from the Dominican Republic in the majors. If someone had told me that in 1958, I would have never believed it.

I am so proud when I see Dominican kids sign and become good players. I hope and pray for them to become good citizens, too, because not only are they going to make good money and be famous, but people will like them.

I started scouting for the A's in 1984 and I stayed with them through 1996. It was an interesting job, but it was sad in many ways because I had to let so many kids go. It was hard, too, because so many things started to happen with the faking of the ages and names. It used to be okay to sign players after high school, and then we switched to 16-year-olds. Sandy Alderson and I used to talk a lot about it, and he asked me what I preferred for the kids. Did I prefer that they concentrate on baseball and forget school? I said no, I thought they should go to school. He said he disagreed with me, and that they should concentrate on baseball so they could become major leaguers more quickly.

In 2010, Alderson was appointed by Commissioner Bud Selig to address the problems of corruption in the Dominican. People were all over him. I saw that the ages of the kids they wanted to sign were getting lower and lower. But then Alderson said there would be a rule that kids had to go to school and they would have to make better grades. I hate to say it, but a high percentage of kids who sign contracts in the Dominican don't know how to read and write. That has to be changed.

It is better for everyone if the kids finish high school and become better educated, even if their career is going to be in baseball. My mother was right about that.

CHAPTER 16

Minister of Sports

*J*uan Marichal gained great satisfaction from his job as scouting director for the Oakland A's in the Dominican Republic. In contrast to when he was a teenager and the chances of being discovered and offered a straight route through the minors to the majors was a matter of stiff odds, he went to work at a time when the landscape had changed.

Although his pitching career ended in 1975, Marichal's Dominican fans never forgot him. He remained a revered figure, and his stature only increased after he was elected to the Baseball Hall of Fame. Unlike being an active athlete, once a player is selected for the Hall of Fame, it is forever.

As scouting director for Oakland, Marichal was again connected to Dominican baseball in a significant way. Who wouldn't want his or her son to be noticed by the great

Juan Marichal? Who wouldn't want the famous Juan Marichal to come to the house, sit around the living room, and discuss their son's future?

Marichal probably could have continued in his capacity indefinitely had he wanted to, despite the emotional upheavals he felt when he had to turn away a young man. However, things changed in the Dominican in a way that lured Marichal into a career change of his own.

Although Marichal has always described himself as being non-political and as someone who does not like partisan politics, he was drawn into the role of what essentially was a ward boss for President Joaquin Balaguer. With a few gaps, between the early 1960s and 1996, Balaguer was the Dominican's chief of state for 22 years. But in 1996, a new president, Leonel Fernandez, was elected. When President Fernandez was filling his cabinet positions, he was struck by an idea.

At that point, Marichal had met Fernandez exactly once. During one of his campaign appearances, Fernandez had attended a local university graduation that Marichal was present at because one of his daughters was in the graduating class. Marichal did not think anything of it. Fernandez won his election and was about to assume office to start his first term as head of the nation. Marichal did not know the man, and Fernandez only knew Marichal through his fame as a pitcher and by his reputation. With no advance meetings or discussions, or any kind of warning, the president sent word to Marichal that he wanted to speak with him. The president did not provide any other information, and he did not mention what the topic of the meeting would be.

Marichal and his wife really had no idea why the retired pitcher was being summoned. He thought there was an off chance, because of his prominence in the country, that the new president wanted to talk to him and invite him to his upcoming inauguration. Of course, all he would have to do was send a written invitation. There would be no reason to have a face-to-face meeting about that. So Marichal was perplexed, but he accepted the invitation to stop by the president's office for a chat.

ONE DAY I GOT A PHONE CALL FROM PRESIDENT LEONEL
FERNANDEZ'S OFFICE. IT WAS HIS SECRETARY CALLING TO
inform me that the incoming president would like to talk to me. I
was very surprised. It was pretty much out of the blue. I told Alma
about the call and told her I didn't know what he would have to
say to me. All I could say was, "Maybe this was an invitation to his
inaugural event."

So I went to my appointment. I said hello and right away he said
to me, "I want you to become minister of sports." Just like that. No
small talk. Nothing else. I said, "Mr. President, I've got to go talk to
my family about it." He said, "Of course you can go and talk to your
family, but please I want you to accept the offer."

He did not give me any details about the job, but I thought I
knew what the job was. He wanted me to represent the government
at international sporting events and that meant more than baseball. It
meant you had to deal with every athlete in every sport in the nation.
Everyone, right from the smallest kid to the athletes in the Olympics,
in every sport. I accepted the job. I had a lot to learn, though, especially about sports I had never followed.

I did a lot of traveling inside the country and internationally. I went
to the Pan American Games. I traveled to Puerto Rico, Colombia,
and Venezuela. We sent athletes to the Summer Olympics in 1996
and 2000. We had a couple of athletes in the Winter Olympics doing
cross-country skiing. But we also developed a lot of programs for kids
at schools, universities, and all levels.

We helped kids get started in many sports. We helped top
athletes, too, the elite athletes. We helped support them so they
could have careers. Except for baseball, there was no money in other
sports. We organized events for different age groups. I think at the

time we focused on developing 12 sports, but later we added about four more.

Of course, baseball was the biggest sport and it was already the most developed because of the majors. There was also boxing, softball, track and field, basketball, weight lifting, table tennis, and tennis for men and women. We don't play much soccer. Just about everyone else in Latin America does. I like soccer, but we don't play much soccer and we don't play much football. You know why I like soccer? Because to play that sport you have to be in top shape, and I think all athletes should be in top shape at all times. Unlike pitching, you won't get a sore arm. You might get a sore foot.

We advanced the sports quite a bit in four years. My job, my mission, was to prepare athletes at every level, at every age. After kindergarten we started sports for kids as beginners, even checkers. We had a lot of good players.

Baseball is what I knew best, but we hired specialists for each sport to spread knowledge, to help everyone. They helped me learn about the other sports, too. I had a lot of fun. It was completely different for me. There was not much baseball in my life at the time. But the sport we had to invest the most money in was baseball. A lot of the people did not have money for equipment. Remember, when I was young we made our balls and bats. So we supplied bats, uniforms, and shoes for kids to play.

We adopted a policy that the government was going to supply every athlete, no matter how young, with the needed equipment to get started in his or her sport.

One thing that was strange for me is that, as part of the president's cabinet, they gave me a car and driver and a bodyguard. Someone had to drive the vehicle. They wouldn't let me drive. I had to have a bodyguard with me, and at my house. That was the first time in my life I had a bodyguard. I had to, but I didn't agree with it. I don't think anybody is going to hurt me. Why would they? There is no reason. I might be wrong, but that's how I feel.

Every time I went anywhere I had two officers with me. It was uncomfortable in the beginning, but then I got used to it. One thing I did was ask them not to wear military uniforms and to wear civilian clothes. That way they could walk with me anywhere and not be so conspicuous. That worked out better.

It is ironic that the biggest danger I experienced was in the car. In April 1998, after I was appointed minister of sports, I almost got killed. We were driving home from giving away equipment at a park near Laguna Verde where I grew up. It was mostly baseball equipment, and that was one of my good times on the job. I got a lot of satisfaction out of seeing the kids when we brought them equipment. I tried to go all over the island to give away baseball equipment.

When we finished for the day, we thought there was something wrong with the vehicle so we decided to stay at my sister's house. But the driver, Bernardino Lopez Ferraras, took the car to a nearby town to get it fixed. He came back to the house and said, "The car is ready. We can go." I was already in bed. I had called my wife and told her I was not coming home and was staying at my sister's.

We should have stayed there. But we left. I was in the back seat and I was sleeping, but I felt the car weaving a little bit and I woke up and sat up straight for a while. I kept looking at the driver. He took his cap off and put it back on. He wiped his face and I kept looking. He drove for another 10 minutes or so and I thought, "Oh, he's fine." I lay back down and went back to sleep.

Near a town about half an hour away, the driver fell asleep at the wheel and drove the car into a ditch off the left side of the road. When we hit the ditch, I woke up. The only thing I could see was the trees coming at us and vehicle lights. I thought the car would lose speed and we would be all right. But it didn't happen that way. Right in front of us was a big overpass made of concrete, and the car hit it head-on. There was no way we could get out of the car.

I almost got thrown through the windshield. I was cut and bruised all over. My shoulder was dislocated. I had a concussion. I was in bad shape.

Somebody from another car stopped behind us and called an ambulance. I was taken to the hospital and somebody there called my wife and told her I had been in an accident. It was three or four o'clock in the morning. Alma said, "No, he's in Laguna Verde. He's with his sister, sleeping over there." She thought I was still at my sister's because I didn't call her back to tell her that we were going. Finally, she came to the hospital early in the morning—with my daughters, my son, and my friends—and I didn't recognize anybody. Even the president came to see me.

After the accident I had so many little pieces of glass in my hair that my oldest daughter, Rosie, came to the hospital to visit every day just to pull the glass out. I was in the hospital more than a week.

When I got out of the hospital I still couldn't move my arm, so I decided to go to Miami to have surgery. But a really good doctor in Miami examined it and told me to exercise it. I said, "Doctor, I can't. I can't do anything with that arm. I can't button my shirt." He gave me a cane to hold in my right hand and to pull with my left hand. He said if I pulled it back and forth in front of me every day, within three months I would be okay and I wouldn't need surgery. It was better in two-and-a-half months.

That accident was a really bad one. All three of us were lucky to be alive. If you saw the car, you wouldn't believe people walked away from it. When the vehicle hit the concrete wall, it went up in the air and came down like it was parked there. I believe the only reason we survived was that the vehicle never rolled over. The other guys were in bad shape, too. The driver was less seriously injured, but his chest was hurt from the steering wheel. My security guard, Eduardo Rodriguez, was hurt. The guys in the front seat got a lot of glass.

I remained as minister of sports until 2000. Athletes got better because of all the help from the government. I don't mean from me, but from the government. The government supplied everything they needed in terms of equipment. But the government also supplied more educational opportunities. I run into some of the athletes now and they say, "I graduated from this or that place when you were minister of sports." I say, "I'm glad."

The same kind of programs have continued since I served as minister of sports. The government spends a lot of money on this. That is something I am proud of doing. We won the right to have the Pan American Games in 2003 in Santo Domingo. That was very big for my country.

Fans in the Dominican Republic think we should win gold medals in baseball every time, but there are a lot of countries that play good baseball, like the United States and Cuba. In the World Baseball

Classic in 2009, fans said, "We have the best baseball players in the world. How come we did not win?"

I have one answer for that, and I don't know if people will agree with me. By having the World Baseball Classic in March, when teams are in spring training, the players are not ready. For the United States, Venezuela, Mexico, Canada, and the Dominican Republic, that's not the right time to have the Classic. In March, those players are never going to be in shape. There is no great time, and that's the problem if major leaguers are going to play. So Cuba, Japan, and South Korea may be on top all the time.

One possible answer is to take two weeks off in the middle of the season, like they do in the National Hockey League for the Olympics, but I don't think the big leagues will do that. Personally, I would rather see the World Baseball Classic played right after the World Series in a warm-weather place in early November.

When I was minister of sports, the government had the money, as well as the commitment, to spend on sports. The Dominican Republic was always a pretty poor country, but now things are getting better. Many of the baseball players who make a lot of money are very generous in what they give back. Other developers have come in to build beach resorts, and that has helped tourism. We have more big hotels along the water, with casinos next to them to bring in money.

There is a lot of new construction going on in Santo Domingo. The community is changing. New buildings are going up, and we have a lot of problems with traffic because of that. But the growth is good for business. I see companies being hired to build more highways and tunnels to ease the traffic. The Dominican is changing for the better. There are more jobs in the community. People can live better.

When I was minister of sports, I dealt with other countries during international events. At the Olympics and other big events, they have sophisticated testing for drugs. When I was playing baseball, we never thought about steroids or taking drugs. I think it is very sad what has happened with baseball. After a while, you think there is nothing you can hear that will surprise you about guys taking steroids, but there have been times I was surprised.

The two guys who surprised me the most were Alex Rodriguez and Manny Ramirez. I just didn't think they were doing it. I thought those two guys were clean and I was wrong.

I don't want to believe this about players, but now everyone is suspicious and they think everyone is doing drugs. Albert Pujols is probably the best player in the world now. He has never been accused of using steroids, but he is asked about it. He told one writer, "I'll give back all of the money I have made with the Cardinals if they found me using steroids." I really liked that answer. After that they left him alone.

What has happened that is so sad is that now anyone who comes up and has success, people are going to think he is taking drugs.

I stepped down after four years as minister of sports. It was an interesting time and I think we accomplished a lot around the country, but that was enough time for me. That was the end of my days in politics. Still, I remain very close to President Fernandez and feel extremely proud of the opportunity to serve my country under his extraordinary leadership. He is a great president, and I campaigned for him during the 2004 and 2008 elections.

CHAPTER 17

Dominican Talent

*W*hen Juan Marichal and the Alou brothers broke into the majors, they were pioneers of Dominican baseball, among the first ever to progress from their island playgrounds to the top of the sport. Marichal outdid almost all Latin players ascending from his home country—as well as Venezuela, Mexico, and Puerto Rico—as he became acknowledged as an all-time great and was voted into the Baseball Hall of Fame.

The passion for baseball in those places was fed by the success, at first, of a handful of Latin American players becoming household names. In turn, they gave back to their home communities, helped local officials build new diamonds, donated money for new equipment to kids who were growing up in poverty and needed a chance, and gave of their own time.

Dominican players returned to their home areas for visits or to live in the offseason, and they conducted clinics for youngsters who idolized them. As years, decades, and even generations passed, more and more boys aged into men, fine-tuned their skills, and were sought out and signed by major league clubs.

Each baseball star who graduated from a hand-to-mouth existence on a rural farm followed a similar path, and each recognized the good fortune that changed and uplifted his life circumstances. In the beginning, and for years, there was a trickle of players discovered by big-league clubs willing to give them a chance to make good. Many signed and stalled out in the minors. Later, many more signed and worked their way into the majors.

There were good players, popular at home when they returned, proud of their accomplishments and of proving the case that the best baseball players were grown in the Dominican. And then, through more opportunity and more hard work, the players got better and better. As the 1980s turned into the 1990s and the 1990s into the 2000s, the best players from the Dominican were among the best in the world.

For more than 50 years, Juan Marichal has been part of and a close follower of the Dominican baseball scene. Drawing upon 16 years in the majors, another 14 years scouting, and decades of observing winter ball, Marichal is familiar with the skills, personality, and history of almost every Dominican player who has advanced from the island to the majors. He has thoughts about almost all of them, too.

He is proud of the sheer number of Dominicans who have made it to the majors in the last half-century, but he is equally proud that other Dominican players have been recognized among the best of their time or the best of all time.

Sammy Sosa, who slugged 609 career home runs and is the only player to hit 60 or more home runs three times, had a highway named after him. It is Route 66, matching his best season home run total, and runs right past the Santo Domingo airport.

Alex Rodriguez is the son of Dominican parents and lived part of his childhood on the island after being born in New York. He is considered one of the best players in the world right now. Many believe he could become the all-time home run leader.

Albert Pujols, who was born in the Dominican before migrating to the United States as a youth, has eclipsed Rodriguez in the minds of many as the best player currently in the sport. After 10 years in the majors, he seems destined to record the best all-around statistics for home runs, RBI, and average.

DOMINICAN PLAYERS BEGAN TO APPEAR IN THE MAJORS IN 1956. OZZIE VIRGIL SR. WAS THE FIRST DOMINICAN WHEN HE came up with the New York Giants at the end of that season. There is an airport in the Dominican named after Ozzie. Good player. Smart player. An important Dominican player.

Since that time, I cannot tell you how many Dominicans have signed contracts with major league teams. There must be thousands. But hundreds have made it to the majors to play, if only for a little while.

Jose Acevedo, from Santo Domingo, was a pitcher for a few years in the 2000s for Cincinnati and Colorado. He won 18 games altogether and is a scout now.

Santo Alcala used to pitch for the Reds in the 1970s. He was tall, like 6-foot-5. He used to throw hard, but he didn't last too long.

Antonio Alfonseca was a relief pitcher for a few different teams. He had six fingers on his hands and six toes on his feet. He might still be pitching in Mexico or with an independent team.

Felipe Alou is a very special name to me. He loved all Dominican players. We always knew he was smart when he was playing and thought he would become a manager. And he did. I think he would have been in the World Series in 1994 with the Montreal Expos were it not for the strike. He got to manage his son, Moises, twice.

Jesus Alou is working as a scout for the Boston Red Sox in the Dominican. So he stays close to the game.

Matty Alou is a very sad story. He is very ill. He has been going blind. He is not doing well. Alma and I love Matty and his wife, Teresa. We go to spend time with them, and sometimes Matty recognizes your voice and sometimes he doesn't.

Moises Alou retired in 2008 after 17 years in the majors. He had a good career. Good hitter. Now he is the general manager of Escogido. In 2009 they won the whole thing—the Dominican title, the winter league, and the Caribbean Series. I have always liked Moises. Everybody in the Alou family is close to me.

Joaquin Andujar was an interesting guy, very flamboyant. He is one of the few pitchers from the Dominican Republic who won 20 games in the majors. I was responsible for bringing him from the St. Louis Cardinals to Oakland. Sandy Alderson asked me to compare Joaquin to another pitcher. That was Mario Soto with the Reds. Mario Soto, what a pitcher, but at that time he had some arm problems, so I recommended Andujar.

Joaquin made the all-star team four times and won a World Series championship with the Cardinals in 1982, but he got into trouble, too. He admitted taking cocaine once and he got a suspension for losing his temper during the World Series in 1985. Oakland gave him a six-figure contract for three years, but he never could pitch when he got there, so my recommendation was so bad.

Pedro Astacio was with the Dodgers and Rockies. He was a pretty good pitcher.

Tony Batista did well after I signed him as a third baseman. He made a lot of money in baseball. He was never a big star, but he played well.

George Bell was a really good hitter for Toronto, a strong hitter. He hit 47 home runs one year and I thought he would do well for a long time. But he dropped off fast. I thought he could have played a couple more years. He was a guy who could be temperamental and sometimes hard to figure out. George is from San Pedro de Marcoris. That is where Sammy Sosa is from, and so many other players.

That place has about 150,000 people, but so many players have come from there. Some writers have said it is like a world record, the number of players from San Pedro.

Adrian Beltre is a guy I missed out on signing. He had a great year for Boston in 2010. He was better than I thought he was. He fooled me. If you are scouting, you will never be right about everybody.

Geronimo Berroa was a good hitter. One year he hit 36 home runs with more than 100 RBI for Oakland. He played more than 10 years in the majors.

There were two Pedro Borbons, a father and son, and both of them were pitchers. The older one pitched in Cincinnati for many years and played on those great Reds teams in the 1970s. He was a relief pitcher with a good sinkerball and he was tough to hit. His son played for almost 10 years but didn't have as great a career.

Jorge Brito was a good looking kid when I signed him. He was a better fielder than hitter. To look at him, you would think he was from the American suburbs or something. With white skin, blond hair, and blue eyes, he didn't look Dominican.

Daniel Cabrera played for Baltimore. He was a right-handed pitcher and had good stuff, but then he got wild. He pitched well for a while and then he lost his control. That cost him. He had some kind of stuff, that guy.

Melky Cabrera did a good job for the Yankees in the outfield, but when they traded him to Atlanta in 2010 he had a lousy year. He was so good with the Yankees. I don't know what happened to him with the Braves.

Robinson Cano, boy, what a ballplayer he is. He keeps getting better for the Yankees. Now he's an all-star. I know his father. His father gave him the name Robinson after Jackie Robinson. I know why he's such a good kid. He was raised the right way. I think he's going to be a star for a long time.

Fausto Carmona is a right-handed pitcher for the Cleveland Indians. He has done some good things, but that's one guy who can be better. If he gets the right coach to teach him, he will do better. He just wants to throw that sinkerball. He can be much better.

Hector Carrasco has been pretty good as a relief pitcher. When I first saw that kid, I thought he was going to be one of the greatest relievers because of his speed and his control, but he never developed all the way.

Rico Carty was one of the first stars from the Dominican when he played for the Braves. He was a great, great hitter. That man was born to hit. He couldn't run but he hit .366 one year and he won a batting title. We're good friends.

I signed Bernie Castro, but he had too many injuries. His back got hurt and the injuries kept coming.

Oh my God, Cesar Cedeño had so much talent. He was a good one. They say when you are scouting you are looking for the player with five tools: hitting, running, throwing, fielding, and power. Cesar Cedeño was a five-and-a-half. He was a very, very good player, but I thought he would have done even better.

Bartolo Colon was such a fast pitcher. What an arm he had. One time he was clocked at 105 mph. He won a Cy Young Award. He was not consistent, though. I think his problem was that each year he got bigger and bigger and bigger. He didn't stay in shape.

I think there are maybe six players named Cruz from the Dominican. Nelson Cruz of the Texas Rangers is from my area near Laguna Verde. He is an outfielder, and he is showing that he will be a very good player. He's still young and had a very good year in 2010.

Johnny Cueto, the pitcher for Cincinnati, got hurt in 2010, but when he came back he looked good. The Reds say they are counting on him to be an ace and I like him. I think he has a good future.

Mariano Duncan was a good fielding infielder, also from San Pedro de Marcoris. If you look at him and see what kind of shape he is in, you would think he should still be playing, even if he is in his mid-40s. He has been a coach for the Dodgers.

Tony Fernandez was a very good player in the majors. He was a good shortstop. He came up through the Blue Jays' academy, one of the first ones. Oh, what a shortstop. He had beautiful hands and was a good hitter with a long career. He won four Gold Glove Awards and made the all-star team five times.

The guy with the longest career was Julio Franco. I don't know how he did it. He was almost 50 when he retired. He played a couple of seasons in Japan, but I think he made a mistake doing that because if he had stayed in the United States he would have had 3,000 hits. He could hit anywhere, anytime. He always was in a position to get good contact with the ball. He was the type of hitter who could drive a pitcher crazy because no matter where you threw the ball, outside or inside, he pulled it. You couldn't figure out how you wanted to pitch him.

Julio had to be one of the oldest ballplayers, but to see his body he didn't look 45 or 50. Maybe 38 or 40, because of the shape he was in. He still looks good.

Cesar Geronimo was a really good outfielder, a member of the Cincinnati Reds' Big Red Machine. He was the only guy on that team who didn't hit very well, but he won a Gold Glove every year. He is a very good man, very nice.

Alfredo Griffin was a great shortstop. He did a lot of work with young people in the Dominican, teaching them the game. He's a coach for the Angels, and it won't surprise me if someday you see him as a manager at the major league level.

Vladimir Guerrero, what a hitter. He doesn't talk much, but he hits a lot. I think he is a Hall of Famer. He has more than 400 home runs, a high average, and a lot of RBI. I think he has better numbers than Tony Perez or Orlando Cepeda, and they are in the Hall of Fame. I was sad when I saw him in the World Series with Texas and he didn't field well in the outfield, so he had to be a designated hitter. I didn't think he looked like himself hitting. Sometimes that can be the pitching, but I think he can still hit and should be able to keep playing. He will have to take less money with a new team, but if he wants to keep playing, he can find a team. It will have to be in the American League as a designated hitter.

Vladimir swings at everything. Inside. Outside. Wherever the pitchers throw it. I tell young pitchers, "Don't worry about him. Throw to him right down the middle. Then he won't swing." With him, you never know.

Julian Javier was one of the first Dominican players to make it big. His first season in the majors was the same as mine, 1960. He was a second baseman with the Cardinals and won two World Series titles. What a gem of a guy. What a human being, all around. He is one of my best friends. When he first made the majors it was because of his fielding, but in the last part of his career he was a pretty good hitter.

Julian was a fast runner, but it didn't always look like it. Going from first to second, it looked as if he were walking, but man he was flying. His son, Stan, also played in the majors. Stan calls me uncle.

Ubaldo Jimenez had his first big season in 2010 with the Rockies. He is a good pitcher and I like him very much. He is young, but you think he is old because of the way he composes himself, the way he acts on the mound. He threw a no-hitter in 2010, the first ever by a Rockies pitcher.

The all-time Dominican home run hitter for games in our country is Felix Jose. I signed that kid and he broke into the majors in 1988. When I shook hands with him, I thought about Willie Mays. He had big hands. He was a switch hitter with power on both sides. He made it to the majors, but he didn't make it big.

We brought Jose Lima to the Oakland Athletics academy. He wanted me to sign him. I was in Oregon at the time, and the two Oakland instructors at the academy let him go. Jose Lima cried when he left. Later, when I came back, he told me he was so sad and he was crying again. We kept up a good relationship through the years, and he did make it.

Jose made it to the majors with the Detroit Tigers and later got traded to Houston. He won 20 games in Houston one year, but he was struggling after that and the general manager there asked me to talk with him. He played for a few other teams, but he was never the same pitcher. He had a lot going on. He liked to sing. He liked to≈entertain the fans, a funny man. But he passed away young in 2010. He was only 37.

Francisco Liriano is a great talent. He has had some bad luck with the Twins, losing games 1–0, 2–1. He could use a little more run support. He had some injuries, too. I think he's got the stuff to be a great pitcher. In 2011, he pitched a no-hitter.

Ramon Martinez is Pedro Martinez's brother. He was really good. He won 20 games once and pitched a no-hitter for the Dodgers. His career didn't last long because he got hurt. His shoulder wore out.

Pedro is one of the best. In all my years in baseball, I haven't seen a guy like Pedro Martinez. He calls me "Papa." He was so good, with a big fastball, even though he isn't a big man. When you look at him on the mound, you think, "There's a pitcher there." You know that he was going to be tough to beat. He was fast, with good control. He wanted to be on the mound. You knew he was the boss out there. He was a master. At the end, he didn't have the speed he once had, but he was so smart that he was still a tough pitcher.

Manny Mota was the greatest pinch hitter who ever lived. He could probably still hit now. Andy Mota is Manny's son, but he had a much shorter career. It seemed impossible that Manny could hit for so long. He took good care of himself, stayed in shape, and worked out. He was ready any time the manager wanted him. Manny has a foundation in the Dominican and he's got a baseball academy with maybe 200 kids. It's not with one team, just a Manny Mota operation to teach kids younger than the ones who would be signed by major league teams. He gives them a head start.

The first time I saw David Ortiz hit, I thought he had a problem because he couldn't pull the ball. He hit everything to the opposite field, to left field. He was playing for Escogido and I told the people with the team, "If a batting instructor grabs that kid and teaches him how to pull the ball, he's going to be a great hitter." He learned to hit to the right side, and what a hitter he became. He has good power and is a good human being. Every offseason, Ortiz brings a lot of major league players to the Dominican to play at softball tournaments and raise money for charity. He brings a lot of big names to the country. A great man.

David had a tough start in 2010. A lot of people criticized him and some wanted him out of Boston. He came back and hit 32 home runs and drove in more than 100 runs to show them he was not through yet. The team picked up his contract option. He got

$12.5 million, but he wanted an extension. They are still worried about him. That's business.

Tony Peña was a catcher in the big leagues for almost 20 years. He used to swing hard at everything, but he was a great fielding catcher with a great arm. He won several Gold Glove Awards. He later became a manager in Kansas City and won the AL Manager of the Year Award. Now he coaches for the Yankees.

Pascual Perez had a lot of talent. He was a showman on the mound, but he wasn't that successful. He got lost driving to the ballpark once in Atlanta. When I was with the A's I wanted to sign him, but the Yankees signed him. He has two brothers who played in the majors, too, Melido and Carlos, but Pascual had the most success. All three were pitchers.

Luis Polonia is very popular in the Dominican. He has been playing winter ball for about 27 years. He was a great player before he gained weight. He hit .300 in the majors, but in our home country he holds every record for hits, runs, and about everything except home runs. He was still playing well into his forties but recently retired.

Albert Pujols, what a player he is. He is from the Dominican but played high school baseball in the United States, and then junior college before the Cardinals drafted him. It seemed like he came out of nowhere to be a star. An incredible hitter. He has the best numbers of any player for the first 10 years of a major league career.

Albert is also a very nice guy. He is a guy you want to be around. I met him in the U.S. first and then in the Dominican. Every year he comes to the Dominican and does things for charity organizations. He was just visiting recently and played in a doubleheader charity softball game. I heard he hit 11 home runs in the doubleheader.

Aramis Ramirez is a good hitter, and he can be important to the Cubs as they rebuild. He was hurt in 2010, but I think he's going to bounce back.

Manny Ramirez is such a great natural hitter with lots of power. He was closing in on 600 home runs. But he has had problems, too. He got suspended for taking drugs and he argued with his manager. Then he failed another drug test in 2011, when he was trying to make a comeback with Tampa Bay. After failing the test he retired. What he has done is wrong. I thought he was a clean player. It really hit me hard when I read that.

He is real friendly with me, but he's so quiet. Sometimes he seems to be in another world.

I wish Manny had been better in the outfield, because at the plate he was one of the best, a special player. He was an RBI machine.

Hanley Ramirez won a batting title for the Florida Marlins. He is a very good shortstop, and I think he will be a good player for a long time. The Red Sox traded him for Josh Beckett and they got Mike Lowell in the trade, too. I don't think you can say it was a bad deal, even if Ramirez is a star. Boston benefited from it, too.

Jose Rijo did a great job pitching for Cincinnati. He was married to my daughter Rosie at the time. In 1990, I was broadcasting as a color analyst for Oakland when the A's played Cincinnati in the World Series. The Reds were about to win in the late innings and they told me to go down to the locker room to get ready. I was in the elevator going down and my boss, Sandy Alderson, was coming in. I felt bad because I didn't want him to think I was celebrating, but I felt good because Rijo was my son-in-law. Sandy saw my face, looked at me, and said, "Juan, go celebrate with your family." I was relieved because he knew I was happy for Rijo. But he was pitching against my team, the team that I worked for, so it was a tough situation. After the game we did go out and celebrate. Jose won two games and was Series MVP.

Alex Rodriguez, in my book, has been the best. I am disappointed about the drugs, and he has battled some injuries, but he can still play at a high level.

Juan Samuel had a great arm and was so fast. He played second base in the majors for 16 years. He was a good player and has been a good coach. He has managed teams in the Dominican and I think he could be a full-time manager in the majors. The Orioles used him as interim manager in 2010 before he went to coach for the Phillies.

Alfonso Soriano has tremendous power. He doesn't look big, but he hits the ball so hard. He has struggled a bit the last couple of years. Watching a guy play so well one year and so poorly the following year is tough to figure out.

When Sammy Sosa was hitting all those home runs in 1998 and he and Mark McGwire were chasing Roger Maris, the whole country was going wild. I thought it was a beautiful thing that went on between them when Sammy would say, "You're the man." People loved that. That summer, it was like it was when Fernando Mania swept Los Angeles. People couldn't wait for the game to start. Every day, it was about who was going to hit that next home run.

Sammy is the only player to hit 60 homers three times. He is big in the Dominican. The president loves him and appointed him as an ambassador. He still lives in the Dominican and Miami. I know there was suspicion in the United States that he took steroids, but he never said he did. Everybody in the Dominican loves him.

Juan Uribe is a great guy to have on a team. He is not a superstar, but teams want him. He started for the White Sox and they won the

2005 World Series. He started for the Giants and they won the 2010 World Series. I watched him late in that 2010 season and he kept everybody happy and loose in the clubhouse, and it was the same on the field. It seems to me he gave 150 percent. You want players like that on your team. He plays hard and he plays to win. You put that guy at shortstop and he does a pretty good job. You put him at second base and he does the same thing. His reward is winning.

Ozzie Virgil is my compadre. We have been friends for a long time. We played for Escogido together in 1958. I baptized his daughter Justine. He is a lovely guy, a very happy man to be around. He is a good instructor and manages in the Dominican and Venezuela. He knows the game so well and can help young players.

If I had to pick my all-time Dominican all-star team as a manager it would go like this: Catcher, Tony Peña. First base, I would have to go with Albert Pujols. Second base would be Julian Javier. Shortstop would be Tony Fernandez. Third base would be Alex Rodriguez. In the outfield it would be Felipe Alou, Cesar Cedeño, and Sammy Sosa. My backups would be Miguel Olivo as catcher, Rafael Furcal, Nelson Cruz, and Aramis Ramirez. Pitchers would be Pedro Martinez, Joaquin Andujar, Mario Soto, and that kid from Texas, Neftali Feliz, in relief. And Rafael Soriano in the bullpen.

I was only a manager for one game. I won that game. It was the MLB All-Star Futures Game in San Francisco a couple of years ago. Hall of Famer Dave Winfield managed the other team. I was the winning manager, so I am retired at 1–0. I have a 1.000 winning percentage.

I think I'd rather be on the pitching staff of my all-star team. Let us have Felipe Alou as the manager. He has more experience doing that, and I was a pretty good pitcher.

CHAPTER 18

Staying with the Game

*A*lthough more than 35 years have passed since Juan Marichal retired from baseball in 1975, he remains a prominent figure in the Dominican Republic and connected to the sport that has been his livelihood.

Because of his Hall of Fame stature, Marichal stays plugged in to baseball and makes appearances at All-Star Games and World Series events. He has mingled with some of the most famous people in the world and has worked as a sportscaster with his own show in the Dominican, and as a broadcaster for the Oakland Athletics and for ESPN's Spanish-language baseball coverage.

When Marichal goes out in public in the Dominican, whether it is for dinner at a restaurant or just walking down the street, he is greeted fondly by fans. Many ask *him to pose for photographs or sign autographs. He does his best to oblige, even when on the move.*

Marichal remains a close observer of baseball in the majors by watching on television and attending select San Francisco Giants events. In the Dominican, he follows his old winter league club Escogido. When Marichal and his son, Juan Antonio (Juanchi), attend Escogido home games, they wear team colors, pulling on Escogido jerseys and caps.

Over the years, Marichal has been honored in several ways by the Giants, including having his uniform number retired and by the raising of a statue in his likeness outside the ballpark in San Francisco. When the Giants reached the World Series in 2010, a group of team Hall of Famers was invited to throw out a ceremonial first pitch. When the Giants won the World Series—the franchise's first since 1954—Marichal was thrilled.

In many ways, large and small, Marichal sees evidence all the time of how fondly baseball fans recall his career. Marichal has been the beneficiary of so many honors he never imagined would come his way that he is eternally grateful for the path that has defined his career and life. As a little boy making his own bat and ball on a farm in Laguna Verde, Marichal just wanted to play the game. He had no idea it could make him so famous and well-off and that his success would turn him into one of the most prominent citizens of the Dominican Republic.

I HAVE COLLECTED A LOT OF SOUVENIRS OF MY BASEBALL CAREER. I KEEP AUTOGRAPHED BATS AND BALLS AND PHOTO-graphs of me with a lot of other baseball Hall of Famers and politicians all in one room at my house. That room used to be a garage, but it is all baseball now.

At one time or another, I have met six presidents of the United States: Richard Nixon, George Bush Sr., George W. Bush, Bill Clinton, Ronald Reagan, and Jimmy Carter.

Ronald Reagan was campaigning for governor of California when I met him. That was a long time ago. I met Jimmy Carter at the Carter Center in Atlanta. I went there with our president. I think he was less of a baseball fan than Bush or his father. I think Jimmy Carter liked farming.

I met George Bush Sr. at an All-Star Game in Denver. He was vice president at the time. He played baseball in college at Yale and was suiting up for this All-Star Game. He was pulling on his socks and said, "I've done a lot of foolish things in my life, but this might be the most foolish."

George W. Bush, who used to own the Texas Rangers, had a dinner for Hall of Famers and I got invited to the White House. I met Bill Clinton when he was doing autographs for his book. He signed one for me and wrote, "To Juan Marichal, my favorite pitcher."

Richard Nixon invited all-star players to the White House when the All-Star Game was played in Washington, D.C. At one time he was talked about as someone who could become commissioner of baseball. I have a picture of me shaking hands with President Nixon. Baseball commissioner Bowie Kuhn is in the picture, too.

I also had my picture taken with Fidel Castro. When I was minister of sports, I went to Cuba to sign a contract with Cuba's minister of sports. It was an agreement that they would help us with instructors for our sports teams leading up to the Pan American Games. It really worked for us.

When I was in Cuba, we sat at a long table with 12 or 14 other people. Castro kept talking to me about baseball and his life and he told me that he used a slingshot just like I did. I knew he had been a pitcher in college and there were stories that major league scouts looked at him. I asked if he could have made the majors as a pitcher. He said, "Yes, I think so. I think I could have made a living out of playing baseball."

After I started playing golf with my teammates on the Giants, I got pretty good at it. I had a five handicap. I won the Hall of Famers golf tournament in Cooperstown twice and I started my own golf tournament to raise money for charity. It has been more than 25 years now.

The best round I ever shot was a 71 at the Santo Domingo Country Club. I got a hole-in-one that day. It's my only hole-in-one. It cost me a lot of money. Any time you hit a hole-in-one you have to buy a drink for everybody in the club that day. That was 16 years ago. I was very proud of my golfing. Now, I don't know. It's not so good. Old age.

I started the Juan Marichal Golf Classic to raise money to help people in the Dominican. The entry fee last year was $400. You get a welcome cocktail party, a gala dinner that President Fernandez and the First Lady attend, and you can win prizes like a beautiful TV set, a bag and golf clubs, musical equipment, a vacation for two. Some of it is donated by the merchants.

I feel proud of what we do for all the foundations we help each January. One time it was in February, but it interfered with the Super

Bowl. Since we wanted to make sure we could bring people from the United States, we do it in January, before the Super Bowl.

I got the idea to start the tournament in 1984. I wanted to invite teammates and players and old friends who played baseball with me who did not know about my country. I wanted people to have the opportunity to see it. I wanted them to understand where I came from.

Mickey Mantle, Brooks Robinson, Catfish Hunter, Johnny Roseboro, Whitey Ford, Bob Feller, Robin Roberts, Orlando Cepeda, and Al Kaline were among the first to come. One year we had seven Hall of Famers. Orlando doesn't play golf, but he did come and joke around. Al Kaline is a good golfer. Ozzie Smith came once and he was one of the best. Barry Bonds came two years in a row, and Chi Chi Rodriguez came. People went wild watching him hit balls and listening to his jokes. Last year's special guests included Pedro Martinez, John Franco, Evan Longoria, and Dale Murphy.

I used to play every year, but one time I had surgery and I couldn't play. I just hit the opening shot, like a ceremonial first pitch, and then I rode around in a golf cart to all the different holes and talked to people. The whole thing takes three days and it's a big party.

One time we gave all the money we raised to a hospital in Santo Domingo, and the next year they invited me to see what they did with the money. They built a lot of new rooms. Another time we gave to a foundation called Learning to Live. It helps educate kids who suffer from diabetes. They all have an illness or a handicap.

Before I die, I will be happy if people say of me that I did something good for other people. I want that. I want to help people who need attention. That's why I organized the golf classic. That was the meaning. I want to be remembered more for helping people than for what I did in baseball.

Soon after I was elected to the Hall of Fame, I was selected for the Hispanic Heritage Baseball Hall of Fame. Additionally, the Giants retired my number. I always wanted number 21, but when I got to the majors someone else had that number and I chose 27. In the Dominican Republic, February 27 is the day of independence, liberation from Haiti. It's a big celebration day. So at that time I liked 27 and it was a special number for me, because that was the date we became a member of the free world.

The day my jersey was retired we had a ceremony down on the field at Candlestick Park before a game. My wife and daughters were there, but the two youngest ones were too young. The team had me raise the number in the air and show it to the fans. Later the Giants shipped me my jersey in a frame.

After the Giants left Candlestick and AT&T Park was built, the team began making statues of famous players and putting them up near the stadium. Giants owner Peter McGowan worked hard to get a statue of me. Every time I went to San Francisco he would talk to me about it. He said, "I don't want to get out of here before I see that statue."

When they chose the sculptor, William Behrends, I had to fly to Miami to meet with him. He took pictures of me and brought in a lot of pictures from the days when I was pitching. The Giants have statues of Willie Mays, Willie McCovey, Orlando Cepeda, and me. Oh, and they have one of a seal—a symbol of the old San Francisco Seals team from the Pacific Coast League.

Behrends made a beautiful statue. I can see that it's me. Now I hear that everybody who goes there has their picture taken with the statue. That is such a big honor. When I went into the Hall of Fame, I said that was my biggest day. I think the unveiling of the statue was my second biggest day. We had so many people from the Dominican there. The president and the first lady were there. Gaylord Perry and Hobie Landrith, my first catcher, were there. It was a long time since I had seen Hobie. Jim Davenport came, and so did Orlando.

I thanked the Giants for building the statue and then I thanked San Francisco for helping me be a good pitcher through the years. I always had a good relationship with the fans, right from the beginning. I almost pitched a no-hitter in my first game. But also, right from the beginning, I used to stop for a half an hour or 45 minutes to sign autographs for the kids.

On the day they showed off the statue at AT&T Park, the Giants wore uniforms that read "Gigantes," which is Spanish for Giants. They did that for me, too. You know what happened? They won the game, so they wore those uniforms one more time. Baseball superstition. I didn't have any superstitions when I was pitching. I just got out there and tried to do the best I could.

Back when I was working in insurance in the Dominican, I got involved in doing a sports broadcast. They came to me perhaps because I was Juan Marichal, a guy who played so many years in the majors. That made me attractive to them. It was a sports show, but I did baseball. They sent me with a cameraman to the United States to interview players, both Dominican and American.

I liked it, but I stopped after I joined Oakland for scouting. After I finished scouting, I became a broadcaster for the A's. A few years ago I began broadcasting for ESPN Deportes, the Spanish-language version of ESPN.

Some years ago, ESPN made a documentary about me. They went all over San Francisco, up the cable car, through the hills, and every-where else. It was very nice. At that time they asked me to work for them, but I said no. They asked me again in 2006 and I agreed. We started with the World Series and the World Baseball Classic, winter ball and the Caribbean Series. ESPN hired me to do the playoffs and World Series, sometimes on the radio and sometimes on TV.

In 2010, they hired me to work during the season and to work the playoffs and World Series. It has been a lot of fun. I got involved in the games again. Earlier in the season the Giants invited me to see some games, so I saw the Giants play in Philadelphia, San Diego, Texas, and San Francisco.

I did not think they were going to win the pennant at first. I knew they had a chance because of their pitching, but for a while I thought San Diego was going to run away with it. Then in September the Padres slumped. The Giants moved into first place and started playing much better ball. San Diego was shaky. The Giants pitched their way to victory.

By then I had met some of their players. I talked to Tim Lincecum, the pitcher, and Buster Posey, the young catcher, and I told him, "You guys can do it. You have the pitching now." And I talked to Juan Uribe and I told him they could get it and he said, "Yeah, we're going to get it. We're going to win." So they did.

For the first game of the World Series, the Giants invited me to throw out the first pitch with Willie Mays, Orlando Cepeda, Gaylord Perry, and Willie McCovey. Only Willie Mays got sick with the flu and couldn't be there. Monte Irvin was there, too. Monte is 92 and was in a wheelchair. We helped him get up and he threw the first pitch. I think that was a great moment, a big moment.

Everyone was on their feet cheering. It was exciting, especially when the game started. To be in that stadium for the World Series, that was something. It felt wonderful to be there.

After the game I was supposed to take my son-in-law and his father to a restaurant that I used to go to all the time on Fisherman's Wharf. Al Scoma, the owner, and I became good friends and we used to play golf together. To get out of the stadium after the game and to catch the vehicle that was going to take us there, we had to walk 15 blocks through the crowd.

Some of the fans were asking for a picture. Some were asking for an autograph. Pictures were okay because they were fast, but autographs take time. We were hungry and we couldn't wait to get to the restaurant.

Then the Giants beat Texas to win the World Series. I knew people would be happy in San Francisco, but oh my God, I had no idea what it was going to be like. I never thought the parade was going to be that large, with more than a million people. I was very happy for the fans. The Giants had never won in San Francisco before. I did not get to win a World Series with the Giants, but I am certainly glad I got to see them win one.

I don't know how long I will keep broadcasting. Maybe one more year. Maybe a few more. I want to enjoy the farm. My wife wants me to sell everything and travel. I don't know if I will sell the farm where I grew up. It was only 50 acres then, but now it is over 1,000. I started buying properties nearby and we grow rice, plantain, bananas, sweet potatoes, and other things.

When I was a youngster, all I wanted to do was play baseball. I liked living on the farm. It wasn't until I was a teenager that I thought I would pitch for any team outside of the Dominican Republic.

The only thing I dreamed of was becoming a baseball player. When I talk to kids today, I tell them that the word *impossible* doesn't exist. If they had seen the village where I was born and grew up, it would be hard to believe that I achieved so many dreams and received so many honors. First becoming a professional baseball player and then ending up in Cooperstown. That's something that is very hard to believe after coming from a little place like Laguna Verde.

At that time, it was very difficult for Latins to play in the major leagues. So you take all of that, and I come to the conclusion that God is always looking at me. Without God, I could never have accomplished what I did.

I have been very lucky. My family is special to me, the people I've met, the friends I have made. It has been a very good life. I'm a happy man.

A Baseball Night
by Lew Freedman

Bucking the traffic successfully as thou-sands of workers exit downtown Santo Domingo at the end of the business day—and thousands more converge around the downtown stadium that is home to Escogido and Licey in the Dominican Winter League—requires either a police escort or a magician for navigation.

Juan Marichal's driver remained relaxed as he steered the boss's car through narrow openings. He identified back ways past parking guards and used little maneuvers that brought Marichal close to a back door of Estadio Quisqueya.

On the way, Marichal, pleased to be attending a game, started talking about one of his favorite topics: how much everybody in the Dominican loves baseball. "It's the No. 1 thing in the country," he said. "It's the thing that everybody cares about the most. Everybody knows the game."

A little walking is still necessary. Marichal and son Juanchi, wearing identical short-sleeved Escogido red jerseys and matching red baseball caps, slither past several small groups of people before fans begin to recognize Juan and hail the Hall of Fame pitcher for his autograph or for a photo.

This happens a lot when Marichal is out in public, and while he is almost always obliging, he also knows the little celebrity tricks about avoiding being surrounded and trying to stay on the move.

Marichal and his party of three were able to enter the ball field through a back gate that accessed Escogido's administrative offices instead of passing through a more crowded public gate past a ticket-taker. After warm greetings with a few team officials in the offices, Marichal was led through the stands by security men and deposited in a field-level box where Escogido general manager Moises Alou watched the team he had assembled for the winter season.

The son of Marichal's long-time compadre Felipe Alou, Moises Alou, then 44, had only recently retired from active major league service. During his 17-year career ending in 2008, Alou batted .303 and was a six-time all-star. The old pitcher and the generation-younger administrator greeted one another warmly.

Both Escogido and Licey are Santo Domingo teams, and the 1955 stadium is home for both squads. It holds about 20,000 fans and seemed about two-thirds full. The teams' proximity to each other makes them natural rivals. Escogido is nicknamed the Lions and Licey is nicknamed the Tigers. From the time he was a teenager, Marichal has been affiliated with or a fan of Escogido, whose own origins pre-date his. The club was founded in 1921.

The Dominican Winter League, probably the highest quality league in the majors' offseason, starts in October and runs to

February. The top teams then compete in the Caribbean Series against the best teams from Venezuela, Mexico, and elsewhere. One of Marichal's earliest broadcasting gigs was doing commentary on the Caribbean Series.

"It looks like a pretty good crowd," noted Marichal as he scanned the stands. "A lot of people wait until the American players come."

Over the years, dating back to Satchel Paige and Cool Papa Bell, many of the finest players in the world have competed in winter ball. The Dominican attracts not only the best players who grew up in the country and feel an obligation to show off their talents for the home folks, but also other major leaguers who are trying to gain more experience or work on developing new skills or staying sharp in the offseason.

Even early in the season, the rosters of Dominican teams are dotted with the names of major leaguers working on their swing, trying to develop a new pitch, or trying to put up eye-catching numbers that will gain them a chance as a free agent.

Licey had jumped to a 4–0 lead before Marichal made it to his box seat behind Alou. As he popped out of a tunnel in the grandstand and walked down a flight of concrete stairs to the seats, heads swiveled and whispers followed. "There's Juan Marichal," many said. Marichal either did not hear or chose to ignore the comments and just kept walking.

Someone asked Alou if he heard much about Marichal over the years from his father and uncles, Matty and Jesus. He laughed. "All the time," he said.

Note is taken when a major leaguer steps up to bat for either team. There's Jake Fox. There's Willy Aybar. Starlin Castro has shipped in from the Cubs. Carlos Gomez, the swift young outfielder for the Milwaukee Brewers, was in the game.

"He's going to be a force," Moises Alou said of the rookie. "He just got here."

The game was being televised and there were probably eight major leaguers sprinkled throughout the lineups, giving the teams name recognition with the fans.

When players on the outskirts of Escogido's dugout got a glimpse of Marichal sitting a few feet away, some tipped their caps.

Periodically, a fan jogged down the stairs attempting to reach Marichal for an autograph or to take a picture. Security discreetly intercepted the person a few sets of stairs north of Marichal's seat. Once in a while the fast-talking individual offered a reasonable explanation of why he had to talk to Juan, or Juan recognized the man and asked that he be allowed to pass. The TV camera had spotted Juan in the stands and by then had probably beamed his image to the nation.

Marichal's cell phone rang and the call was from his ESPN Deportes broadcast partner, who was in the house. He wanted to know if he could hook Juan up at his seat for some guest commentary about the game. Juan agreed but also said, "I think we've been on TV already."

Technicians and a cameraman came to provide Marichal with earphones and a microphone and to monitor the technology that would allow Marichal to be a guest color man without leaving his seat.

Between innings the mascot of Escogido and the mascot of Licey, a tiger and a lion, got into a mock rumble, with the fans taking sides consistent with their general rooting interests.

At the end of a half inning, a group of attractive young women danced to rousing music on top of the Licey dugout across the field.

Each squad had its own dance team, and the Escogido bunch had the same amount of foot-stomping energy. There was one difference. When the Licey girls danced, the nearest players' eyes were riveted to their gyrating backsides. When the Escogido girls danced, the players in the dugout turned completely around, ignoring the field, and stared at the fetching lasses until they finished wiggling.

If Marichal had a TV comment on these goings-on, they were lost in translation. This was a whole new look for color commentary. Marichal sat in his box seat next to the Escogido dugout, barely elevated from the plate, the on-deck circle almost close enough to reach out and touch, and he talked for a few innings. He could have chosen to sit in an enclosed press box but preferred to be closer to the action, out in the pleasant, 75-degree night air and with the crowd.

Unfortunately from a rooting standpoint, Marichal's club fell behind early and was never truly in the game, losing 8–4.

Marichal said he was a little surprised by how many major league players had begun playing so early in the winter season after only a short rest from their regular season. More would be coming in December, a few weeks ahead, he knew.

Throughout the evening, Marichal bantered with Moises Alou, a few visitors from the stands, and son, Juanchi. The Marichals were asked if they wanted a cold drink, and Juan was looking for diet soda. He has diabetes and generally watches his diet carefully. When his Diet Coke arrived, Juanchi appropriated the container to read the nutritional information. He okayed the contents before letting his father have it. He was watching out for Dad.

After the game, the Marichal party adjourned to one of the pitcher's favorite restaurants, in his mind the best place to eat meat when he is in Santo Domingo. The unexpected name of the restaurant, worth a chuckle to Americans, was Davy Crockett, and it had an American Old West decor. The owner must have watched Disney when he was young, been a Fess Parker fan, or studied the lore of the Alamo.

Since it was a late-night dinner, only a few other tables were occupied, but the diners at one small table and the group of eight at another table recognized Marichal. One man at the large table said hello to Marichal and then told baseball stories to his dinner companions. After the initial wave of hellos, no one interrupted Marichal's dinner as he ordered, conversed with guests, and ate. A celebrity of similar magnitude in the United States might have had trouble swallowing a forkful without strangers intruding on his meal. Marichal ate his steak and baked potato in peace, talking baseball between bites.

Marichal explained how his life-long allegiance to Escogido began. When he was a boy, he rooted for a different team, Aguilas. But when he was in his late teens and ready for a breakthrough in his career, it was Escogido that showed interest. Someone he knew told him that another observer had bad-mouthed him to Aguilas and that's why that team wouldn't give him a tryout.

Talk turned to the famous Marichal-Warren Spahn game in 1963 that lasted 16 innings. Juanchi, as the youngest of six children, was too young to see his father pitch in person, and there was neither the interest nor the prevalence of technology for every baseball game to be taped and archived 40 years ago. More than anything, Juanchi would love to see a video of the Spahn game. However, there is no indication that such video exists. He has only seen snapshots of Marichal pitching—a slice of cake, one could say, when he wants to devour the whole thing.

Early on, Juanchi discovered that being the son of a celebrity in the Dominican can be a mixed blessing. Yes, you might get to hobnob with famous people such as President Fernandez. However, the occasional awkward situation does arise. One day when he was younger, during a visit from the president, Juanchi was going through his baseball cards while they were both waiting for his father.

Juanchi showed off an old Mickey Mantle card he had, his favorite, and to his shock and dismay the president said, "This is for me? Thank you." "No!" Juanchi declared. Afterwards he felt bad, and on a subsequent trip to Cooperstown for the annual Hall of Fame induction ceremony, Juanchi obtained two Mickey Mantle autographed baseballs and gave one to the president.

Marichal told another story that involved Mickey Mantle. In the late 1950s, the Washington Senators had a pitcher named Pedro Ramos from Cuba. Ramos loved the American West and he gave into his flamboyant inclinations, wearing a cowboy hat and cowboy boots and driving a Cadillac. One time, Marichal said, Ramos was pitching in relief for the Senators against the Yankees in a critical situation and struck out Mantle to escape danger.

Ramos took the ball and tossed it to a batboy because he wanted to save it. After the game, Ramos asked the batboy to take the ball to the other clubhouse and ask Mantle to autograph it. Mantle was very nice and he signed the ball, Marichal said.

A day or so later in the same series between the teams, Ramos was again in the game in relief and Mantle came up to the plate again. This time, Mantle hit a ball so hard and so far for a home run that according to Marichal it might still be traveling. He joked that the ball might have landed on a train and gone hundreds of miles. Anyway, no one knew how far the ball went or where it landed.

After the game, Mantle signaled to the batboy, gave him a note for Ramos, and sent him to the Senators clubhouse. The message to Ramos read, "I would ask you to sign the ball, if you can ever find it." Marichal laughed uproariously at the story, his eyes twinkling.

As Marichal stood to leave, the man at the head of the table for eight stood also and shepherded the old pitcher to his own dinner guests for a hello. Marichal continued talking baseball after the man gave a monologue about Marichal's career achievements with the Giants. Decades after the fact, the man was still incensed that Marichal had not been voted the Cy Young Award instead of Dean Chance in 1964.

Marichal seemed less upset. He had long before come to terms that he had not won a Cy Young trophy for a combination of reasons. For one thing, for the first several years of his career the sport gave the award to only one pitcher in both leagues, not one in each league. Also, when Marichal had his best seasons, there was always another pitcher who had a career year.

As his driver moved slowly through Santo Domingo's now-darkened streets, with residents home for the night and turning out the lights for bed, Marichal reflected on a career of greatness with the San Francisco Giants. There had been seasons of more than 20 wins, seasons of stingy earned run averages, All-Star Games, the World Series, a no-hitter. And all of those good pieces added up to something very special, a place in the Baseball Hall of Fame.

The man with the high-kicking delivery had left his mark on the sport he loved and on the country he loved. Whereas once Marichal had been an anonymous poor boy on a farm, his dazzling pitching skill made him one of the most beloved citizens in the Dominican Republic. It was good to be Juan Marichal. Even in the half-darkness in the back seat of a car, it was easy to read his pride.

Appendix

JUAN ANTONIO MARICHAL
Nickname: Manico
Born: October 20, 1937, in Laguna Verde,
    Monte Cristi, Dominican Republic
Throws: Right
Bats: Right

Minor League Pitching Statistics

Year	Team (Class)	W–L	W Pct.	ERA	G	CG	SHO	IP	H	ER	BB	SO	WHIP	SO/BB
1958	Michigan City (D)	21–8	.724	1.87	35			245.0	200	51	50		1.020	
1959	Springfield (A)	18–13	.581	2.39	37	23	8	271.0	238	72	47	208	1.052	4.43
1960	Tacoma (AAA)	11–5	.688	3.11	18			139.0	116	48	34		1.079	
	Total, 3 Seasons	**50–26**	**.658**	**2.35**	**90**			**655.0**	**554**	**171**	**131**		**1.046**	

Major League Pitching Statistics

Boldface numbers = league leader

Year	Team	W-L	W Pct.	ERA	G	CG	SHO	IP	H	ER	BB	SO	WHIP	SO/BB
1960	SF Giants	6–2	.750	2.66	11	6	1	81.1	59	24	28	58	1.070	2.07
1961	SF Giants	13–10	.565	3.89	29	9	3	185.0	183	80	48	124	1.249	2.58
1962	SF Giants	18–11	.621	3.36	37	18	3	262.2	233	98	90	153	1.230	1.70
1963	SF Giants	**25–8**	.758	2.41	41	18	5	**321.1**	259	86	61	248	0.996	4.07
1964	SF Giants	21–8	.724	2.48	33	**22**	4	269.0	241	74	52	206	1.089	3.96
1965	SF Giants	22–13	.629	2.13	39	24	**10**	295.1	224	70	46	240	0.914	5.22
1966	SF Giants	25–6	**.806**	2.23	37	25	4	307.1	228	76	36	222	**0.859**	**6.17**
1967	SF Giants	14–10	.583	2.76	26	18	2	202.1	195	62	42	166	1.171	**3.95**
1968	SF Giants	**26–9**	.743	2.43	38	**30**	5	**325.2**	**295**	88	46	218	1.047	**4.74**
1969	SF Giants	21–11	.656	**2.10**	37	27	**8**	299.2	244	70	54	205	**0.994**	3.80
1970	SF Giants	12–10	.545	4.12	34	14	1	242.2	269	111	48	123	1.306	2.56
1971	SF Giants	18–11	.621	2.94	37	18	4	279.0	244	91	56	159	1.075	2.84
1972	SF Giants	6–16	.273	3.71	25	6	0	165.0	176	68	46	72	1.345	1.57
1973	SF Giants	11–15	.423	3.82	34	9	2	207.1	231	88	37	87	1.293	2.35
1974	Boston Red Sox	5–1	.833	4.87	11	0	0	57.1	61	31	14	21	1.308	1.50
1975	LA Dodgers	0–1	.000	13.50	2	0	0	6.0	11	9	5	1	2.667	0.20
Total, 16 Seasons		**243–142**	**.631**	**2.89**	**471**	**244**	**52**	**3507.0**	**3,153**	**1,126**	**709**	**2,303**	**1.101**	**3.25**

Postseason Pitching Statistics

Year	Series (Result)	Opp.	W–L	ERA	G	CG	SHO	IP	H	ER	BB	SO	WHIP	SO/BB
1962	World Series (L)	NYY	0–0	0.00	1	0	0	4.0	2	0	2	4	1.0	2.0
1971	NLCS (L)	PIT	0–1	2.25	1	1	0	8.0	4	2	0	6	0.5	–
Total, 2 Series			**0–1**	**1.50**	**2**	**1**	**0**	**12.0**	**6**	**2**	**2**	**10**	**0.67**	**5.0**

Career Rankings
(through 2010)

Category	Major Leagues	San Francisco Giants
Wins	53	3
Losses		5
Winning Pct.	50	15
Earned Run Average	132	18
Games Started	75	2
Complete Games	88	6
Shutouts	18	2
Innings Pitched	70	5
Batters Faced	81	5
Hits Allowed	105	5
Earned Runs Allowed	157	4
Strikeouts	45	2
Walks	349	6
Hits per 9 Innings	142	16
Walks per 9 Innings	56	4
Strikeouts per 9 Innings	253	22
Walks + Hits per IP	18	3
Strikeouts/Walks	28	1
Home Runs Allowed	39	1

All-Star Games
(bold = starter)
1962 (1), 1962 (2), 1963, 1964, **1965**, 1966, **1967**, 1968, 1969, 1971

Hall of Fame Voting
(75% of vote required for induction)

Year	Votes	Vote%
1981	238	59.4
1982	305	73.5
1983	**313**	**83.7**

Index